finding me

a journey of self-discovery through a cancer diagnosis

amy ewald

FINDING ME: A journey of self-discovery through a cancer diagnosis

Copyright © 2022 Amy Ewald.

All rights reserved. No part of this publication may be reproduced, distributed, or transmitted in any form or by any means, including photocopying, recording, or other electronic or mechanical methods, without the prior written permission of the publisher, except in the case of brief quotations embodied in critical reviews and certain other non-commercial uses permitted by copyright law.

ISBN:
978-0-473-64623-3 (paperback)
978-0-473-64625-7 (ePUB)
978-0-473-64626-4 (Kindle)
978-0-473-64627-1 (PDF)
978-0-473-64628-8 (Apple Books)

Cover design by Sarah Johnson.

Interior book design by Praditha Kahatapitiya.

Cover photo by Trev Hill Photography.

First printing edition 2022.

www.amyewald.com

Scripture taken from the HOLY BIBLE, NEW INTERNATIONAL VERSION®. Copyright 1973, 1978, 1984 by International Bible Society. Used by permission of Zondervan. All rights reserved.

WHAT READERS ARE SAYING

"This book was one of the rare ones where I couldn't and didn't want to put down until I read the very last page. It was deeply engaging and captivating; it also satisfied my curiosity for the Asian migrant journey. I found myself transported into Amy's little world of a mother living an ordinary life with extraordinary fortitude in the face of unexpected curve balls in life and allowing good to come out of it. One could relate to her challenges and suffering even if the circumstances are different. A feel-good inspiring story, narrated through the lens of humour at unexpected moments."

— Dr Felicita Fedelis,
Senior Lecturer, University of Malaya

*"***Finding Me** *is an honest story. Amy writes in a way that connects with the audience immediately. From the first page, you'll feel genuinely invited to join her on this journey, and you'll feel like you're right there with her — even when you don't want to be. There are moments that paint cancer in a realistic, miserable way, which may make the reader uncomfortable (itchy, shall we say?). In a world where everything is supposed to be padded and packaged, I am grateful Amy didn't hold back. Therefore,* **Finding Me** *has everything you would expect from a nitty-gritty cancer story. However, the one thing I didn't expect from such a raw retelling was the encouragement. Not only does Amy let you see inside her day-to-day suffering, she also takes you on a beautiful journey which shows you a cancer diagnosis through faith."*

— Lance Mosher,
Author of Transformed: A Spiritual Journey

"There is a saying I think of often when considering the future. It's from Proverbs in the Bible, chapter 16, verse 1: We can make our plans, but the final outcome is in God's hands. Amy, inviting us into her journey of self-discovery with kindness and grace, illustrates this wisdom with exquisite storytelling. It's raw. It's hard to read at times. It's beautifully heartfelt. It was effortless to find myself sitting in the various scenes she described — whether a doctor's office, a kitchen table, a clinic, or an airplane with two toddlers. I'm grateful for Amy's willingness to share this story and genuinely hope that countless people discover courage and inspiration in the pages of **Finding Me**."

— J Paul Fridenmaker,
VP, Generosity and Network Relations, TrustBridge Global Foundation

"Having a family history of cancer and seeing my brother's journey with it, **Finding Me** reminded me of the courage and uniqueness of every person who is diagnosed with cancer. The struggle and heartache, the known and the unknown. The grace that we are given by God when traveling through these valleys of life and death. This story held me captive and left me wanting to know more."

— Shaun Vining,
Pastor, City Impact Church Balclutha

"Every book reveals a story of the person who wrote it and I've never felt more connected with an author than I've been with Amy. She clearly states at the beginning that **Finding Me** is not about cancer and I can assure you that it is a hundred per cent true. I love the candid, clear and even funny way she wrote it. You don't have to go through cancer to relate to this book ... You just need to be human. I highly recommend that you not only read it about Amy but also about you; because it is about you. THANK YOU, Amy, for your bravery and vulnerability in sharing your personal story. I wish more people have the courage you had, not only to fight your battle but also to share it with the world and recognize and honour God's work on you in the midst of it all."

— MINOR ARIAS,
MINDSET & BUSINESS COACH

"**Finding Me** by Amy Ewald is a profound memoir. First of all, I have yet to meet someone who felt relief at receiving a cancer diagnosis! I had not quite imagined that what is often portrayed as grim can still bring balance and clarity to one's world. Amy pours herself onto the pages. She recounts how the diagnosis journey also became a journey that shaped her identity and outlook. She realised what mattered most and how to navigate life based on the many hats she wore — a wife, mother, daughter, sibling, friend and colleague. The book sheds light on the real, raw, humour-filled, and also sobering encounters many of us overlook when those near and dear to us are walking through trying seasons. It's not just a book about cancer; it is a book about life, understanding how to navigate and remaining rooted in the wake of unexpected news. I highly recommend this!"

— EUGENIA MAREMBO,
BLOGGER AND PUBLIC POLICY ANALYST, NSW GOVT

In loving memory of Granny.

To all the Grannies of this world: Your granddaughters' lives are largely influenced and moulded by your love.

TABLE OF CONTENTS

Author's Note xi
Introduction xv

PART 1: MALAYSIA
Chapter 1: Till We Meet Again 3
Chapter 2: The Seven-Year Itch 21
Chapter 3: The Last Leg in Malaysia 37

PART 2: NEW ZEALAND
Chapter 4: The Plight of Eczema Sufferers 49
Chapter 5: Alternating Between Job and Job's Friends . . 67
Chapter 6: The Bump in the Road 83
Chapter 7: Talk About Perfect Timing 105
Chapter 8: The Cancer-moon 121

PART 3: THE HOSPITAL
Chapter 9: 8C, The Oncology Ward of
    Dunedin Hospital 139
Chapter 10: Pride Is a Difficult Pill to Swallow 155
Chapter 11: The Importance of Preparation 167
Chapter 12: The End of the Beginning 179

Afterword 189
Resources 191
An overview of my treatment plan 193
Acknowledgements 197
About the Author 199

AUTHOR'S NOTE

Thank you, dear reader, for picking up this book. The road to writing it has been anything but straight and easy. The only word that can describe this book is 'God-birthed'. The idea to write my story was planted by friends and family, and initially, I laughed it off. But it slowly took root and didn't seem like an impossible task after a while.

This book was written to fill a largely unexplored niche in cancer journeys: the actual discovery and diagnosis. During this phase of the journey, so many questions arise that are unaddressed in general literature, such as:

- Are the symptoms I'm experiencing cancer symptoms?
- Should I seek a doctor's advice when my symptoms are so trivial?
- What do I do if I think I have cancer, but my doctor doesn't seem to think so?
- How do other people feel when they're waiting for a diagnosis?

My hope is that you'll better understand the discovery journey after reading this story.

However, this is not a story that will apply to all cancer patients, nor is it written solely for cancer patients.

In essence, it's not about cancer at all.

This is a story of **personal and spiritual growth**, written for anyone and everyone who has struggled with doubt, fear and anxiety at some point in their lives.

It is a story of a journey toward a life-altering discovery and the subsequent thoughts and feelings that follow such a revelation. It is a tale of self-discovery: of finding oneself and one's identity and what one can do with that discovery. Do I like who I am? Do I change if I don't? Why am I resisting change?

Keep in mind that this book is a character study, an in-depth look at the experience of ONE individual (that is, me) on the journey of cancer discovery and the mental, emotional and spiritual growth that accompanied the process. Some of the names have been changed to protect the privacy and rights of those involved in this story.

The statements I make in this book are based on my beliefs, my culture and my identity. You may or may not agree with all my views, but I pray you keep an open mind and allow me this avenue of sharing without fear of offence. I am open to and welcome discussions on different viewpoints. If you feel strongly about something I've mentioned in this book, do get in touch with me.

If you are reading this book seeking the details of my cancer treatment, you will be highly disappointed. Consider yourself warned. If, however, you can live without knowing what the actual treatment is like, I promise you an entertaining read and a heartfelt narration of how a life-altering discovery can change an individual for the better.

I've cried a bucket load of tears writing this story. Throughout the whole process, I've grown and drawn closer to God in a way that I could not have imagined possible. Our relationship now has a new depth that was previously lacking. This story is therefore dedicated to Him. The words may be written by me, but I couldn't have written this alone. To God be all the glory.

If you are a believer like me and you enjoy this book, I urge you to praise and glorify Him. May this story bless your life in the way He wills it to.

If you are not a follower of Christ, I hope that as you read this, you at least believe that a greater force or power was at work in me as I wrote these words. I pray that my faith shines through the pages and piques your interest in this God that I keep mentioning. He has blessed me tremendously, and I hope this story of mine will, in return, be a blessing to you. If you ever want to get to know this God that I love and am trying to walk with daily, I'd love to connect with you.

Without further ado, I present you my journey and testimony. Happy reading.

Blessings,
Amy Ewald

INTRODUCTION
THE BEGINNING OF EVERYTHING

Have you ever had one of those itches that annoyingly presents itself as a mild tingle? You reach out to scratch it, but nothing happens. You try again, but this itch seems to be under the skin. So you dig your fingernails in to give it a really good go but try as you might, the tingle just won't go away. You frantically claw at that patch of skin with every fibre of your being, but the horrible sensation persists no matter what you do or try. The only relief you get is to continue scratching to the extent your skin turns raw and bleeds. Even then, the moment you stop, the itching resumes.

Now imagine that localised, single itchy patch occurring all over your body. A relentless sensation of irritation from head to toe that won't subside. This persistent full-body itch is what I experienced *on a daily basis* for six months prior to my diagnosis. But I'm getting ahead of myself. Let's backtrack a little to the time my journey began.

PART 1

MALAYSIA

CHAPTER 1

TILL WE MEET AGAIN

Early August 2019

I tapped the red phone icon on WhatsApp and stared at my phone for the longest time. My shoulders slumped with the weight of the news my parents had just told me. My mind raced with a thousand thoughts — the things I had to do, the planning and arrangements we needed to make.

Can I take time off work?

How long would I/we go for?

Do we have the money for this?

What about Rod? He definitely won't be able to take time off at such short notice.

Should I go alone? Who would watch the kids if I did?

All these questions, none of which I had real answers to. However, the thought that stood out above all the others was the one thing my parents told me over the phone mere minutes ago.

"We think you should come home to see her and say goodbye."

Her being my maternal grandmother.

My grandmother was born in China in 1926. She was brought to Malaysia (then known as Malaya) as a child and adopted by a local family. I don't know the full details of why she had to leave China or how she came to reside in Malaysia, but China was going through a period of civil unrest during her childhood years, so I can only hazard a guess that this was why she left. Fortunately for her, the family she was adopted into was quite well-to-do and provided her with nothing but the best, education included. One of the things that surprised Rod (my husband) when he first met my grandmother was the fact that she spoke fluent English, a rarity for someone her age who didn't grow up in a country where English is the main language.

My grandmother entered into an arranged marriage during her teenage years; the nuptials were expedited due to the Japanese occupation of Malaya in 1941. However, the marriage did not last. In later years, my grandfather left her for another woman, leaving my grandmother to raise nine children on her own. Talk about a financial dilemma! But my grandmother was a strong woman. She had to put food on the table somehow and was now the sole provider for the household. She couldn't leave home to work full time due to her children, so she played to her strengths and brought the work home — she nannied. Luckily for her, there were no limits to childcare numbers then, unlike today's regulations. She and her family wouldn't have been able to survive otherwise.

Chapter 1: Till We Meet Again

Shortly after my brother was born, my grandmother moved in with us. Both my parents worked full time in order to support us, a fact that my brother and I will forever be grateful for. However, the lack of a stay-at-home parent meant we had to search for an alternative solution for our household needs. My brother and I were very fortunate that my grandmother agreed to help with childcare. She raised my brother and me to be the fine individuals we are today (and as you can see, humility was one of the many traits she instilled in us).

One of my earliest and fondest memories of my grandmother is of me helping her iron. Now that I think about it, I was no help whatsoever. It wasn't all my fault, though. The 'iron' she provided me with was a little rectangular broken alarm clock.[1] I could never understand how her shirts turned out so crisp and smooth, whereas the little handkerchief I was charged with stayed so rumpled no matter how hard I pressed. If you're chuckling at this image, remember that I was only around five and gullible.

The other memory I have of her that really stands out is her doing the laundry on a little scrubbing board.[2] My grandmother was convinced this was the way to wash clothing properly. She had no trust in machines that, in her opinion, just swirled clothes around in dirty water. What was

---

1 *When I was young, little plastic battery-run clocks were a common household item.*

2 *If you've never seen one, google 'laundry board'. People used to use these to do their laundry. Beating up laundry with wooden sticks was a thing, too; apparently it really helps with the cleaning.*

that going to achieve? While she scrubbed and viciously beat at the laundry, I would sit on a stool a little distance away and recite my times tables. We even had occasional quizzes, where she'd suddenly ask, "What's five multiplied by nine?" and I would answer as quickly as I could.

Thank you, Granny. You're the reason I know my times tables back to front even today.

So, when I spoke to my parents that day in August, I knew I had to return to Malaysia. Granny's health was rapidly deteriorating due to age. All her life, she had been very careful with food and supplemented her diet with nutritional pills. She never had serious illnesses, apart from the occasional ache in her back that came with heavy lifting and bending (children can be heavy!). Recently, however, her health had begun to decline after years of hard labour. Her heart was failing. She had suffered a series of mild heart attacks that weakened her heart and caused her respiratory distress. Her doctor believed it was only a matter of time. Even more devastating was the fact that her usually sharp mind was starting to fail. That, more so than the weak heart, crushed us all.

In our fragile human state, the mind plays a very important part in shaping a person. When someone's mind fails, the person you know and love disappears. They gradually lose their personality, their memories and the special things that make them who they are. Not by their own volition, but due to gradual loss of brain function. That was the case with my grandmother. At the time of my parents' call, she was experiencing hallucinations and paranoia.

Chapter 1: Till We Meet Again

When someone's mind fails, the person you know and love disappears.

She was losing her memory and accusing my parents of poisoning her. My parents were giving her medication according to the doctor's orders — pills for her weakened heart and various other pills designed to prevent adverse incidents from occurring rather than treating a specific condition. However, as she was refusing to take them, my parents resorted to crushing her pills and dissolving them in her drinks or sprinkling them in her food. My grandmother noticed and was refusing to eat in fear of being poisoned. This was making her weaker than ever. She was waking up to eat in the middle of the night to make up for the lack of food during the day. Basically, she was surviving on sandwiches. This really was no way for a 93-year-old to live.

My parents made the difficult decision to put her into a home. It was at this point that they decided to ring me and tell me to visit — to pay my respects and see my grandmother before she forgot me entirely. I also wanted to introduce my children to their great-grandmother before she forgot about their existence and for her to see Holly (my youngest), whom she had yet to meet.

It is important to note here that in my family, we have what some may consider a different approach to funerals and saying goodbye, in that they did not expect me to return to Malaysia for my grandmother's funeral. It would be nice but definitely not expected as funerals were for the benefit of the living, not the deceased. If I wanted to spend time with and ultimately say goodbye to Granny, it was imperative that I made this trip while she was still alive.

If I wanted to spend time with and ultimately say goodbye to Granny, it was imperative that I made this trip while she was still alive.

Still, there were life arrangements to be made. My parents had not seen their grandchildren for over a year, and if we were flying all the way to Malaysia, it was important that they got to spend quality time with the children. After a whole lot of prayer, discussion and life-arranging, the decision was made. Rod and I decided that I should go back with the kids and that we would spend approximately three months with my parents. I took a leave of absence from work, put my business on hold, pulled the kids out of daycare for a few months and booked our flights. Within 48 hours, we were all set to go back to Malaysia.

Chapter 1: Till We Meet Again

A week and a half later

If you have never taken several long-haul flights with two toddlers by yourself, then take it from me: don't do it unless you absolutely have no other option. As much as I love my children, the 26 hours we spent together travelling was not exactly quality time. It was excruciating, exhausting and mentally draining. In the week prior to flying, I went on a shopping spree, buying colouring books, sticker books, miniature toys, snack foods, little backpacks for them to carry their soft toys in, safety wrist harnesses (disclaimer: I really don't enjoy using these as they resemble dog leashes, but we had to prioritise their safety) and everything else I could think of that would make the trip easier.

I was a strong-willed woman. This was a piece of cake. I was ready!

Boy, was I wrong.

The trip started out well enough. Rod had taken the day off work to drive us to the Dunedin International airport. We made it with over an hour to spare, checked in the two suitcases I had stuffed with anything and everything we could possibly require for our stay, and took the kids to the little indoor playground where the slide commanded all their attention. Soon enough, it was time to board. This was when things started to go south. Try explaining to two toddlers that Daddy isn't coming along on our family trip, even though he's at the airport. It's like waving a bone in front of an untrained dog and telling him he can't have it. Needless to say, the tears and 'But why?!' started.

Ten minutes later, the tears finally stopped, and the cuddle-kiss-high-five cycle began. We'd move one step towards the departure gate only for Holly to run back to Rod for a "Last kiss, Mummy. Last one!" Lucas, not wanting to miss out, would then run back for another cuddle. We must have had at least ten rounds of this. Finally, I gave Rod a final kiss (this is where I should admit that I had my fair share of lasts too) and headed to the automatic doors, a backpack over my shoulders and a toddler in each hand. The doors opened; I stepped forward bravely and marched out the door like a young soldier heading to battle. Onwards and upwards!

I had barely taken ten steps when a gust of bitterly cold winter wind smacked me in the face and almost made me lose my balance. Right on cue, Holly started wailing. Lucas's face scrunched up and his lower lip started to tremble. With a swoop, I scooped Holly up into my arms.

"We're almost there, darling." I coaxed Lucas while tugging on his wrist.

"You're a brave boy, aren't you? Walk quickly, sweetheart. We'll be nice and warm in a few minutes. See that big plane over there?"

It felt like I was trying to pull his arms out of their sockets, poor boy. After what seemed like an eternity of begging, persuading, threatening, pulling and dragging, we finally made it to the plane only to encounter ... steps.

Narrow, slippery, metal steps, with handrails conveniently located at adult height.

Great.

Chapter 1: Till We Meet Again

Another round of coaxing and half-dragging ensued up the long flight of steps. The passenger walking behind us had the patience of a saint, bless him. We finally made it into the plane. After locating our seats, I removed our backpacks and jackets and settled the kids into their seats with a sweet treat (aka a bribe) each. I sat back and heaved a sigh of relief. When it came time to put the seatbelts on, Lucas declared vehemently, "I don't want to!" Holly echoed the sentiment because, well, just because.

We managed to settle this debate in my favour reasonably quickly, thanks to the lovely flight attendant who came around and put her 'stern' face on. Thankfully, the rest of the flight went by rather uneventfully. We landed in Christchurch just before noon. I looked out the window in dread.

There was no air bridge in sight.

Resigned, I put the kids' jackets and backpacks on. We proceeded to replay the boarding process, only this time in reverse. Thank God, we made it to the warm terminal building without mishap. We had about an hour to spare before our next flight, so I bought the kids some hot chips from Burger King while we waited. We video called Rod, blew him a few more kisses, and by then it was time to head towards the departure gate. I put the kids' backpacks on their backs, slung mine over my shoulders, and put the kids' leashes — er, safety harnesses — on.

It was here that I realised something I had previously overlooked. We'd brought along three cumbersome, heavy, grossly oversized and absolutely useless items on this trip.

Our winter jackets.

We couldn't leave them behind at Dunedin because we needed them for the two-minute walk on the tarmac back at the airport, but we had no need for them from this point forward and definitely no need for them in Malaysia![3] I was now stuck hauling the three thick jackets while travelling across continents with my toddlers. Sighing, I draped them over my right arm and started walking.

We had barely taken five steps when Holly tugged on my hand and piped up.

"Mummy, poop."

Sigh.

"Okay, honey, let's change your nappy; there's a toilet here."

Easy, I thought. *This will take two minutes.*

Unfortunately, this was not the case — thanks to the wrist harnesses. Rod and I loved them when we bought them, especially the double Velcro. "It's an additional safety feature! Easy enough for adults to undo, but they prevent children from taking the harness off easily," the in-store salesperson told us enthusiastically. "The harness is also long enough and stretches so you don't have to take them off for every single thing."

That sold it. The more safety and convenience features, the better! However, no one told us that they weren't designed to

---

[3] *Malaysia is a tropical country located close to the equator. There are only two seasons in Malaysia: 1. Hot and dry, and 2. Hot and wet.*

Chapter 1: Till We Meet Again

be used in conjunction with a backpack on your back, much less a backpack and two toddlers.

We went to the family change room where I thought it would be a simple matter of just changing the nappy. The harnesses were long enough that I wouldn't even have to undo them, right?

Wrong.

I tried to shrug the backpack off and found myself in knots. Literally. I couldn't pull my arms out unless I undid Holly's harness.

Ah well, it's just one.

I was wrong again. I unfastened Holly's harness, but then I couldn't swing the backpack around to reach the nappies unless I broke Lucas's arm! Reluctantly, I disconnected the other harness as well. Did I mention these had double Velcro on them for safety purposes?

Safe? Definitely. Convenient? Definitely not.

To Lucas, the unfastening of his harness meant we had reached our destination. He made himself comfortable, took off his backpack, unzipped it and started rummaging through it. By the time I finished changing Holly's nappy, he was already halfway through a snack — in the changing room right next to the toilet bowl. It took me another ten minutes to pack up his mini picnic, stem the flow of tears, put all our backpacks on, redo the harnesses and heave the winter coats onto my arms. It was a good thing I had left plenty of time for us to board the flight.

Fortunately, the flight to Melbourne was pretty uneventful. Our arrival was, however, a little delayed, leaving us only a few minutes to catch our connecting flight, which was (of course) departing from the other end of the terminal building. I had to run, dragging poor Lucas behind me and carrying Holly and the stupid, useless winter coats in my arms. Lucas cried, Holly wailed, and we finally got to the gate to be told that our flight was delayed.

Thank God!

I was relieved but also slightly annoyed that I'd subjected my toddlers to the massive rush for naught. After two hours of waiting, we finally boarded and were on our way to Singapore, where we had the longest transit time — approximately six hours.

Normally, the Singapore airport is a hive of activity. It's not known as the best airport in the world for nothing. There are various entertainment lounges, numerous eateries, shops, an outdoor garden, a swimming pool and the world's tallest airport slide. Changi International isn't just an airport; it's also a tourist attraction. However, due to the timing of our flights, we landed in Singapore at 1 am. Almost everything was either closed or running at reduced capacity. It seems even the best airport in the world has down times.

The airport staff member who met us at the plane entrance after we disembarked was extremely helpful. He handed me a trolley with a capsule for Holly and helped us to the transit counter, where we received our boarding passes for the last leg of our trip to Malaysia. The flight wasn't until 7 am, however, so he led us over to some deceptively comfortable looking seats[4] and left us there to fend for ourselves. He looked sorry yet relieved to leave us there. There was literally nothing else he could do for us. Well, actually, he could have offered us the use of their exclusive lounge! Really, the service you get these days.

The kids and I made ourselves comfortable on the seats, watched some early morning cartoons, and snacked our way through their backpacks until it was time to board. We finally landed at the Kuala Lumpur International Airport at 8:10 am (local time). After lugging the backpacks, winter jackets and cranky toddlers off the plane, we strolled towards the baggage claim area. The end was in sight!

But alas, things were not meant to be.

Thirty minutes later

I was staring at an almost empty baggage carousel. Our bags, which I had painstakingly packed, were nowhere to be found. Holly and Lucas were both in tears. They were sweaty, tired, hungry and over the whole adventure. I wanted to scream in frustration as I hauled our hand luggage and two crying toddlers to the lost baggage department (which was, of course, at the opposite end of the arrival hall). By the time I reached the office, I was sweating like a pig.

---

4   *They weren't comfortable enough to sleep on after over 12 hours of flying, trust me.*

I explained our situation and was given several forms to fill out. Luckily, the office was air-conditioned, and the kids quieted enough for me to write down my details. I thanked the officer, sent a silent prayer to heaven that our baggage would be found promptly and proceeded past the automatic doors where my brother was patiently waiting for us. I had never been happier to see him. His first words to me, however, almost cost him his head.

"Where's your luggage?"

I glared at him. The poor man, it really wasn't his fault. Good thing my brother understood and forgave my mood.

I was thrilled when we finally made it to my parents' home, where I could put my feet up and leave the children to my mum and dad, who were overjoyed to see them.

Alas, the next day, instead of the relaxing, rest-filled, gastronomical day I had imagined, my mum and I had to make up for lost luggage by hauling the kids out shopping. I couldn't leave them at home and go alone as both Lucas and Holly hadn't seen my parents for ages. They weren't comfortable being left alone with their grandparents just yet. So out we went, as jet-lagged as I was, to shop for necessities with two toddlers who had no patience or interest whatsoever in clothing. I purchased only the bare minimum in hopes that our bags would be found and delivered soon. My prayers were answered that very evening, as I received a call from the airport staff notifying us that our bags had been found and were *en route* to my parents' place.

A few days later, my parents, my kids, and I made the trip to where my grandmother was staying. It was a clean, tidy little place, a combination of several residential buildings that had been converted into a rest home. At the time of our visit, Granny and the other residents were sitting outdoors in a semicircle around the wall-anchored TV for some entertainment and fresh air.

I teared up the moment I laid eyes on my grandmother. She was a shell of the person I once knew. Granny was always slim, her physique shaped by hard, physical labour, but this woman I saw was skin and bones. It wasn't rational, but somehow, I'd expected to see the same lean, strong woman that I knew and remembered. I didn't recognise the person before me.

A living skeleton.

I quashed that thought the moment it popped into my head, ashamed to even think of Granny that way. I moved closer to this woman, who I knew was Granny and yet wasn't. She was hunched over with her head held up by her hand and her elbow leaning on the arm of her wheelchair. She looked as if she was dozing; her eyes closed peacefully. The only indication she was still alive was the low rise and fall of her chest.

My mother touched her lightly on the arm.

"Mum, Amy and your great-grandchildren are here to see you!" She shouted in Cantonese, her volume at a decibel that could have raised the dead.

I almost jumped out of my skin. Strangely, Granny and the other residents barely stirred. Dad looked at me and offered a sad smile.

"She can't hear very well."

I approached my grandmother, crouched down and grasped her free hand in mine, my eyes brimming with tears.

"Hi Granny, I've missed you," I whispered.

Granny stirred and her eyes opened. They were glazed over as if she had just woken from a long nap. She started crying and mumbling in Cantonese, and I leaned in to listen to what she had to say. A massive lump in my throat emerged and my eyes blurred over when I deciphered the words that she repeated over and over (translated as best I can): "I don't even have the ability to die".

A massive lump in my throat emerged and my eyes blurred over when I deciphered the words that she repeated over and over (translated as best I can): "I don't even have the ability to die".

Somehow, she knew and understood the predicament she was in.

I tried to get her to look at Lucas and Holly, who both looked terrified at this elderly lady who kept crying and mumbling. They managed to give her a small smile and wave (bless them), but if Granny recognised them, she gave no indication of that. I barely managed to contain my tears throughout, but I didn't want to break down in front of the children or my parents.

Chapter 1: Till We Meet Again

We sat there in silence for a while, with me holding and staring down at my grandmother's hands. Those wrinkly, bony, veined hands that had done so much physical labour raising so many children by herself all those years. After what felt like forever, but I'm sure was only several minutes, my dad spoke.

"I don't think she recognises you or the children."

It was a heartbreakingly sad visit.

When it was time to go, the children waved goodbye, and I took her hands in mine for what I knew would be the last time. I whispered, "I love you very, very much", and we went on our way. There was nothing more I could do for or with her, it was all in God's hands now.

I didn't realise it then, but that short time with Granny was a little sneak peek of a confrontation with my own fragility and mortality. In a few months, my whole life was going to be turned upside down.

CHAPTER 2

THE SEVEN-YEAR ITCH

I was itching. There was a prominent bump on the back of my right hand that wouldn't stop itching. I also had sparse, tiny bumps of irritation on the bend of my elbows, the back of my knees, ankles, heels and the arches of my feet. To alleviate the itch, I scratched. However, the more I scratched, the more I itched.

In this instance, my extensive background in science provided the knowledge but no concrete solution to my problem. I realised that in order to stop itching, I needed to stop scratching. The way scratching provides relief is by sending low levels of pain signals to the brain, which overrides the itch sensation. However, these pain signals stimulate the release of serotonin, a feel-good hormone that resets the itch signal. Intense scratching exacerbates this feedback loop, resulting in a never-ending cycle.

The only reason I could think of for my plight was the intense Malaysian heat. It had to be heat rash. After all, it was only three weeks ago that we were in New Zealand, where the average temperature was in the single digits. On the other hand, Malaysia, being a tropical country, was averaging in the 30s.[5] My body was acclimatising to the drastic change and continually sweating to cool itself down. Although my parents' home was well insulated and cooler compared to the outdoors, I was unaccustomed to the overall ambient temperature. In short, it was hot.

I took cold showers to combat the heat and found that the cold soothed the irritation. I also turned to air conditioning to aid my sleep every night. My poor parents, I can only imagine what their power bill was like! Despite the cooling aids I had at my beck and call, I couldn't fall asleep until the wee hours of the morning when exhaustion took over.

My sleeping pattern perplexed my parents. My inability to sleep at a decent hour meant I couldn't be alert for my toddlers when they woke at six. My mum started calling me out for staying up late watching TV, which I was, in fact, doing. It was a good way for me to pass time. I could catch up on my favourite TV shows and distract myself from the sensations that crawled through my body. However, I didn't think this was a detail I needed to share with my mother, so I bit my lip to prevent myself blurting out the reason for my insomnia. They didn't need to know about something so trivial.

To compensate for my absence in the mornings, my parents developed a little routine with Lucas and Holly.

---

5   *These references are in Celsius. In Fahrenheit, NZ was averaging 35 degrees whereas Malaysia was measuring in the 90s.*

Chapter 2: The Seven-Year Itch

They went for daily morning walks and watched the sunrise together while I had a lie-in. Unfortunately, the additional hour or two did little to help. I was only getting three to four hours of sleep each night and the sleep deprivation started showing in my interaction with the children. I would nod off during the day. My mood also took a downturn. I became snippy, and I'm ashamed to admit that my children bore the brunt of this change.

Thankfully, I had my parents. Unaware of the itch that plagued me, they probably reasoned that the abrupt change in time zone and location, seeing Granny's plight in person, as well as Rod's absence, were taking a toll on my emotions. They took on more and more parenting duties, which allowed me to take some time off for myself, something generally unheard of while solo-parenting two toddlers.

I was immensely grateful and grasped at the opportunity to take little excursions out on my own. I spent afternoons strolling the nearby malls and watching movies at cineplexes. The air-conditioned interior of these buildings eased the itch and kept me occupied. I was fortunate enough for this to be a win-win situation; I gained some 'me' time while my parents were able to spend time with their grandchildren, whom they hadn't seen in over a year. I believed that once my body acclimated, life would go back to normal.

Unfortunately, things only got worse.

Two weeks later

"My arms and legs are really itchy! I'm not doing this on purpose. I can't sleep!"

There was an awkward pause. I'd snapped due to exhaustion and frustration.

My parents looked at me as if I'd grown another head. I bit my lip and looked at the floor to prevent myself from further outburst. Feelings of guilt bubbled up inside me. It wasn't my mother's fault. She didn't know I had trouble sleeping because I hadn't told anyone about my condition. She had just told me in no uncertain terms that I needed to get more sleep at night because my nocturnal habits were affecting my days.

I sighed, looked my mother in the eyes, and apologised. Taking a deep breath, I explained my situation and showed them the bump on my wrist and little rash spots on various parts of my arms and legs.

"It's not as bad during the day, especially when I'm occupied. The nights are the worst. I usually fall asleep at around three in the morning when I can't keep my eyes open anymore."

My parents looked at me, the concern obvious on their faces.

"I think it might be the heat," I said defeatedly.

My parents nodded sympathetically. They had been to New Zealand several times and knew that the drastic change in temperature could be a difficult transition. It was fortunate that Lucas and Holly seemed to adapt reasonably well and showed no signs of discomfort.

Chapter 2: The Seven-Year Itch

"Why don't you go see a doctor?" my dad advised. "You've been itching for a few weeks now. Maybe a doctor can prescribe you something that will ease your discomfort."

So off I went.

At the doctor's office
"Oh, that's scabies," the doctor announced nonchalantly.

"Oh, that's scabies," the doctor announced nonchalantly.

I looked at him incredulously.

Scabies?!?! What did he mean, scabies? How could he be so matter-of-fact about it?

I racked my brain as I tried to recall the little I knew about scabies.

* *Note: I couldn't remember much, so the information below is a combination of what I remembered as well as my googling efforts after the visit.*

Scabies, also commonly known as the seven-year itch — gee, this explained why the itch wouldn't go away no matter what I did — is a skin condition caused by a minuscule mite (*Sarcoptes scabiei*) that burrows under the skin. Scabies is contagious and spreads through close physical contact, such as hugs and handshakes. It can also spread via indirect contact; for instance, when one touches a surface, for example, bedding or furniture, that has been in contact with an infected person. For this reason, scabies spreads easily in institutional environments with communal facilities such as nursing homes and extended care medical centres.

The primary symptom of scabies is intense itching. The itching is caused by the live mites burrowing tunnels under the skin, as well as the presence of the eggs that they lay. Scabies also presents several visual symptoms: red streaks on the skin that mark the burrowing of these mites and a red rash that is a result of the body's immune system reacting to both the mites and their eggs.

Scabies mites are very misunderstood, the poor things. They are often thought to be present in lower socioeconomic environments and the slums, where hygiene is often an issue. That is not true. Scabies is not due to unhygienic practices. Scabies can infect even the richest, cleanest and most hygienic person on earth. The only requirement is contact with someone who has it or contact with a surface that has been touched by an infected person.

Scabies is treated using an anti-scabies emulsion that is applied all over the body. The mites can also be killed with oral medication, but this route of administration is reserved for the more severe cases. The tiny problem (pun intended) with treating scabies is that it takes a reasonable amount of time for the symptoms to disappear. The itching caused by the mites does not cease immediately upon application of the medication, regardless of the topical or oral route of administration. The reason for that: the eggs, mite waste and dead mite bodies remain in the skin until the old skin layers slough off and the skin regenerates. As skin cells are renewed approximately every four to six weeks in adults, the symptoms remain for approximately the same period of time.

If the itch does not subside after a few weeks, then it is to be assumed that one or several minuscule mites managed to escape annihilation and reproduce.

The treatment would need to be applied again. Rinse and repeat.

In short, there was no quick way to know if the treatment worked. The only thing one could do was have faith and trust that it did. That, and possess a great amount of patience while waiting for the process to bear fruit.

I didn't know this at the time, but this was the practice run God wisely used to prepare me for the long journey ahead.

I didn't know this at the time, but this was the practice run God wisely used to prepare me for the long journey ahead.

The doctor proceeded to ask me a series of questions in a mix of English and Malay, the national language.

"Where have you been in the last few weeks? Have you visited any crowded places, any rest homes…?" he trailed off and looked at me expectantly.

Rest homes? I thought. My mind immediately zeroed in on the visit I had with Granny. I told the doctor that my grandmother was in a rest home and that we'd visited not too long ago.

"That's probably it!" he exclaimed, seemingly pleased with himself for pinning down the source of infection.

"There's also a chance you may have caught it on your travels. All it takes is one surface and one mite," he continued thoughtfully as if giving me more options would make me happier. I sighed, both frustrated and relieved.

On the one hand, I was glad that I had a diagnosis. On the other hand, how bad could my luck be? My parents and the kids were fine, so I wasn't too worried about Granny or any of the older folk being infected. In fact, I was sceptical of the rest home being the source of infection. I'd probably picked it up from one of the many airport seats or flights that we were on.

I muttered a silent prayer of thanks that neither Lucas nor Holly had any symptoms despite me being in such close proximity to them daily. It was a blessing in disguise that I had been sleeping in a different room altogether as a result of my nocturnal routine. My contact with them had also been drastically reduced due to my parents taking over their primary care.

"Alright, what do I do from here?" I asked the doctor.

"It's easily fixed. I'll prescribe you some anti-scabies treatment. Make sure you apply this all over yourself, from the back of your ears down to your toes, for three consecutive days and also on the seventh day from today. The first three days' applications are designed to kill the living mites. The application on day seven is to kill any remaining mites or the ones that hatch after the third day," he said, scribbling on a prescription pad.

"Be sure to leave the medication on for a full eight hours each time to allow it to take effect. The best way is to apply it prior to bedtime, leave it on overnight, and wash it off in the shower the next morning."

It was going to be tedious, but I could do that. Unfortunately, he wasn't finished.

"You'll need to air your mattresses and pillows to rid them of any mites. Put them out in the sun if you can. Strip your bed and wash the sheets, pillowcases, blankets, towels and your clothes; anything that you've used. Wash them in warm water."

My mind almost exploded with the enormity of the situation. My parents lived in an apartment building. They only had a little balcony where they could hang their laundry out to dry.

How was I supposed to sun the mattress and all the bedding out on that tiny balcony?

I managed to remain silent and just nodded in acquiescence.

He signed his name at the bottom of the script, tore it off the pad and handed it to me. I looked at it wordlessly. The anti-scabies treatment he prescribed me was benzyl benzoate. From memory, it was a foul-smelling, light-sensitive and toxic chemical.

Ewwww.

"You'll have to treat your children too, just in case," he continued in the same nonchalant manner he'd given his diagnosis.

My head snapped up violently.

"What?!?" I blurted loudly.

It was a bit rude, but I was shocked.

"If you have scabies and have had close physical contact with your children, there is a high chance they're infected too. They may not be showing any symptoms yet, but you don't want to wait until it's too late. It's better to treat them at the same time. I can't prescribe their medication because they aren't present, but you can purchase anti-scabies medication from any pharmacy."

I gaped at him in horror.

It wasn't the purchase of the medication I was worried about; it was the application. The doctor looked really young, like he was barely out of medical school and young enough not to have children. Did he realise the enormity of what he was telling me to do? How was I supposed to medicate my children from head to toe and keep them happy in the process? I seriously doubted that they would willingly subject themselves to a slathering of foul-smelling medication. How was I supposed to prevent Holly from ingesting the poison? She was only one and in the habit of putting everything she could lay her hands on (including her own hands) into her mouth!

It was my worst nightmare.

Chapter 2: The Seven-Year Itch

I left the doctor's office with a heavy heart. After collecting my script and purchasing two bottles of anti-scabies emulsion from a nearby pharmacy, I got home and shared the news of my diagnosis with my parents. My parents decided they were at low risk of contracting scabies from me and were happy to forego their treatment. Together, we stripped the beds, did a few loads of laundry, and proceeded to perform a deep clean of the house and, more importantly, the room I was sleeping in. Thankfully, my parents believed in washing machines. I would have just bought new sheets if they told me that I had to use Granny's old laundry board.

That night, I was Catwoman. I had to be silent, stealthy and quick so I didn't wake the children. I stripped them, removed their overnight nappies and slathered them from head to toe with permethrin, the anti-scabies treatment I procured from the pharmacy. I felt like a proficient martial arts warrior, dodging flailing arms and powerful leg kicks, all the while praying they stayed asleep despite the groans and cries of protest. I wasn't confident that I managed every surface, but done was better than perfect. By the time I finished, I was bathed in sweat. In comparison, applying the medication to myself was a piece of cake. It was most fortunate that the kids' treatment only required two applications (on the first and seventh day) compared to my four.

A week after our first treatment, I medicated us all thoroughly with what I thought would be our last application. After my second Catwoman attempt, my eyes teared up in relief. This ordeal was over, and the itch would soon subside.

Thank the Lord!

But I was wrong.

Another two weeks later

The itch was not subsiding. In fact, it got worse. My rash was more prominent, and I now had clusters of red spots on the back of my thighs, as well as on my extremities. I wanted to tear my hair out in frustration. I had done everything the doctor told me to. Surely the itch should have dissipated by now!

The only silver lining throughout this ordeal was that both Lucas and Holly remained asymptomatic. The only conclusion I came to was that I'd made an error in applying the treatment. Perhaps the benzyl benzoate I was prescribed wasn't as effective as the permethrin I purchased for the children. There was only one thing to do, and that was to undergo another course of treatment.

Resigned, I bought enough permethrin to medicate myself and the children for the second time. We proceeded to replay the events of the previous weeks. Perhaps it was practice or my increased agility, but I managed to get away with fewer kicks and smacks compared to the first time. Then it was back to playing the waiting game.

However, my skin and condition showed no improvement as time passed. My itch was still stubbornly present, and the rash spread to other parts of my body like my torso and the sides of my thighs. I was getting tired and frustrated at this stage. My sleeping patterns were not improving, and my mood deteriorated in proportion to the amount of sleep I was getting. It was time to pay the doctor another visit.

By the time I got in to see the doctor the second time, I'd been itching for almost six weeks. This time, I found myself in consultation with a female doctor and explained the situation. I told her that I'd been through two full courses of treatment and that I'd been researching scabies treatments on Google. My research had unearthed the possibility of rare cases of treatment-resistant scabies that could only be treated by oral medication, so I inquired about the possibility of an oral treatment script. Even if my infection wasn't a treatment-resistant version, I was convinced that oral medication would ensure rapid and effective annihilation of the mites.

My doctor, however, was sceptical.

"It is really uncommon for scabies infections to remain unresolved after two rounds of topical treatment," she said, reaching for my hand.

"This doesn't look like a classic scabies rash either," she continued, inspecting my rash carefully.

After several minutes of studying the bumps, she reached for the phone sitting on the corner of her desk. "I think it's best for us to get a second opinion. I'll see if I can reach the dermatologist." She dialled several numbers on the keypad.

I muttered a quick, silent prayer of plea. I really wanted this ordeal to be over!

After several moments of silence, the call was answered. The doctor briefly explained my situation to the clinician on the other end in a low, quiet tone. I waited hopefully, praying that the unseen doctor had a solution to my problem. A few minutes later, she hung up and smiled at me.

"The dermatologist has had a last-minute cancellation and can see you for a physical consultation right now."

"Now? That's amazing, thank you so much!" I replied.

Armed with directions to the department, I grabbed my bag and proceeded to the other end of the medical centre where the dermatologist was located. I was thrilled about being seen on such short notice. The national health system in Malaysia is so busy that there is usually a waiting period of a few weeks, if not months, for an appointment with a specialist. To be able to consult with a dermatologist that very day without an appointment was truly divine intervention. There was no other explanation.

I arrived at my destination and gave my name to the receptionist on duty. I felt like a VIP as I was immediately whisked in to see the specialist, who was expecting me. He listened to my tale attentively and examined the multiple areas of rash on my extremities thoughtfully. I mentioned my treatment-resistant scabies hypothesis and inquired about the oral treatment that was prescribed in severe cases. To my disappointment, he told me that although my information was accurate, severe cases were so rare that the drug was not readily available in Malaysia. The application process for this drug (ivermectin) was lengthy and required extensive paperwork. Unfortunately for me, I didn't meet the requirements in my current condition. My heart sank when

I heard the news. However, he had an alternative diagnosis for me that would explain the inefficiency of my previous treatments.

"Do you have sensitive skin?" he asked, peering at a particularly angry patch on my wrist. "This looks like eczema."

I was taken aback. "I don't think so…?" I answered hesitantly. "I've never had any significant skin conditions as far as I can remember, other than this one." I looked down at my rash. "Is this what eczema rash looks like?"

"Eczema can present itself in many ways and forms. It's different for each individual. You mentioned having several applications of different anti-scabies medications, which are, in essence, insecticides. They're harmful, poisonous and can cause skin irritation. It's possible that the scabies rash has resolved, and this more aggressive rash is due to an allergic reaction to those treatments."

That made sense. I'd had numerous applications over the past four weeks, and I'd seen the poison and irritant warning labels on the bottles.

Great. I had solved one problem just to create another.

His diagnosis made complete sense. This explained why I was the only one in our household itching. If it were a case of severe scabies, both Lucas and Holly would have caught it by now, considering how they needed their daily dose of mummy cuddles and kisses.

"Alright, so it's eczema. What should I do?" I asked.

"There isn't a cure for eczema. In your case, your skin was probably traumatised by the harsh treatments and is reacting to it. We can't cure it, but you can certainly reduce the symptoms by moisturising regularly. I'll write you a script for some fatty cream. You're welcome to use any normal moisturiser but be aware of added scents or colouring as you want to reduce your exposure to chemicals."

He swivelled in his chair to face his desk and started scribbling on his writing pad. "I'll also prescribe you some antihistamines and topical steroids, which should help bring the rash and itch under control."

I was relieved. Here was an answer. It wasn't a definitive one by a long shot, but his reasonable explanation came with an actionable solution, and for that, I was thankful.

"Let's arrange to meet again prior to your return trip to New Zealand. We can see if your rash has improved then. I can write a letter explaining your condition that you can take home to your general practitioner (GP) if it's needed," he said.

We made a follow-up appointment for a few days before our return flight. I thanked him for his assistance, collected my medication from the hospital pharmacy and left for home.

CHAPTER 3

THE LAST LEG IN MALAYSIA

In the weeks following the eczema diagnosis, I moisturised religiously. My skin had never been so cared for. Armed with daily doses of antihistamines and applications of steroidal cream, I vowed to conquer the rash and itch. I was convinced that the dermatologist was right and if I followed his advice, this would soon be a thing of the past. Life returned mostly to normal, save for two very slight and seemingly unrelated health hiccups.

The first one was a mild but persistent cough. I associated this with the haze in Malaysia. Every year, from about May till September, natural as well as manmade forest fires are a common occurrence due to the hot and dry climate. These fires are prominent in both Malaysia and the neighbouring country, Indonesia. Exacerbated by the lack of rainfall, the air pollution is dreadful and shrouds the country in haze.

Coincidentally, 2019 (the year we visited) was one of the worst years in haze history.[6]

Haze particles affect the heart and lungs and are known to cause respiratory illnesses. I reasoned that the constant tickle in my throat was due to this. The haze also added a level of complexity to my efforts to keep my skin moisturised. These air pollutants are known to irritate the skin and exacerbate skin conditions such as eczema. To prevent my condition from worsening, I stayed indoors as much as I could. On our excursions, the kids and I minimised our outdoor activities and kept to indoor, air-conditioned malls.

The second physical annoyance I developed was a peculiar one. I would, very occasionally and with no warning, experience a sudden, lightning-sharp sensation across my left lower back. These sudden sensations were excruciating but lasted for only a few seconds. There was no rhyme or reason to these occurrences. They were not caused by a certain posture, time of day or activity. The sensation appeared and disappeared at the drop of a hat, at random times of day and locations. I kept these painful incidents to myself, brushing them off as bizarre but trivial events. It wasn't until my dad saw me grimacing in pain one day that I mentioned them to him. He came up with a perfectly reasonable explanation for these episodes.

"They sound like muscle spasms. You're constantly lifting Lucas and Holly. They're getting older, bigger and heavier.

---

6   At the time of writing, Wikipedia had a standalone article on the '2019 Southeast Asian haze': https://en.wikipedia.org/wiki/2019_Southeast_Asian_haze

Chapter 3: The Last Leg in Malaysia

You're also doing double the parenting duties at the moment to compensate for Rod's absence."

He was right. At that stage, Lucas was three and Holly almost two. They were growing physically at an exponential rate, and their Dutch heritage did not help.[7] All the heavy lifting was probably straining my back. My dad came to the rescue with a solution. The kids were not going to like it, but they would have to use their little legs more often.

"Lucas is capable of further distances now, and we can put Holly in the stroller when we have longer walks. You need to give your back a little break from all the lifting."

Slowing the passage of time was like grasping at straws; it truly was an impossible feat.

My heart broke a little. As their mother, I wanted to carry my babies for as long as I could. They are little for only such a short time, and although lifting them was physically taxing, I treasured the cuddles they desired. Slowing the passage of time was like grasping at straws; it truly was an impossible feat. Nevertheless, I'd tried to lessen the effects of time by increasing my weight-lifting capacity. However, if my dad was right, the constant lifting and carrying were not doing me any

---

7   *Random fact: Dutch men are said to be the tallest in the world. I didn't just marry a tall man; I married one from the country that produces the tallest people. Well, the consequences had come to bite me in the butt, or back I should say.*

favours. Resigned, I promised my dad I would consciously encourage Lucas and Holly to be more independent.

With the rash, cough and back issues explained, the kids and I enjoyed the remainder of our trip to Malaysia. We spent quality time with my parents and my brother, visited with family and friends, ate our way through all the Malaysian food and delicacies, and had a blast! I was busy and distracted enough during the day to disregard my physical discomforts. The nights, however, were a different matter altogether. Every night I would toss and turn until I fell asleep from exhaustion. This continued in the weeks leading up to Nikki's visit.

Dr Nikki has been a friend of mine since our young, eager days as post-graduate students at the Victoria University of Wellington. Nikki remained a friend even after we both graduated and has been 'aunty Nikki' to the kids ever since they were born. Lucas and Holly love aunty Nikki and enjoyed her visits when we lived in Wellington. Although we were now living in the South Island, Nikki had stayed in contact and visited occasionally. She knew about our trip to Malaysia, and coincidentally, had planned to be in Malaysia as a part of her trip to Asia while in between jobs. We had agreed to meet up if we could.

Nikki came to stay with us at the beginning of October, our last month in Malaysia. The kids were ecstatic to see aunty Nikki, and I was delighted to catch up with a friend I hadn't seen for quite a while. She regaled us with tales of her travels around the continent, and I listened, captivated and envious. It had been a very long time since I travelled independently as an adult (read: sans children). Rod and my travels of late were

Chapter 3: The Last Leg in Malaysia

filled with kids' activities and tailored to accommodate the children's schedules. As amazing as the children are, I missed the freedom of travelling without them.

"Why don't you go somewhere for a few days with Nikki?" my mum asked one day. We were sitting around the table, talking to Nikki about her upcoming travel plans.

My dad nodded in acquiescence.

I experienced a split second of euphoria before I clamped down on my emotions.

"I can't," I said mournfully. "The kids wouldn't cope without me for so long."

Go away for a few days without the kids?

It sounded like an impossible dream. I love my children, but like all toddlers, they could be hard work and needy. Having my parents around was a major help, but there were still things that Lucas and Holly wanted me to be present for and help with — for instance, when they had trouble sleeping when they were overtired — just because I was Mum. Although things had improved during the time we were in Malaysia,[8] leaving them alone with their grandparents, even just for a few days, was out of the question.

It was, wasn't it?

I brushed the thought away, but the idea had been planted in my head. The more I considered it, the more enticing and

---

8   Lucas and Holly had grown to know and love *poh poh* (Cantonese for grandma) and *kong kong* (Cantonese for granddad). Note: the words sound exactly as you read them. Cantonese is an ideographic dialect of the Chinese language and is not written using the Latin alphabet.

FINDING ME | 41

plausible it sounded. It wasn't long before I brought the matter up for discussion again.

"They want you constantly because you're here. If you're not physically present, they will be happy to deal with whomever they're familiar with. Children are adaptable, they will adjust just fine," my mum reassured me.

Did I mention that my parents are awesome and that I appreciate them?

So, Nikki and I made plans, and in the middle of October (three weeks before the children and I were due to leave for New Zealand), we flew to Seoul, South Korea. The four days we spent exploring the city and its surroundings were truly an amazing break, both mentally and physically. It was great to have some adult time with a friend for a change. Touring a city without children also meant that we could visit tourist attractions that required extensive walking without hesitation. Both Nikki and I clocked a very healthy number of daily steps on our smartwatches during this trip!

The South Korean autumnal weather provided relief for my lungs and skin. The air was haze-free, which resulted in me coughing less, and the cool temperature soothed my irritated skin. Weary of the constant heat and humidity in Malaysia, Nikki and I stood out like sore thumbs walking around Seoul in the evenings wearing only a single layer of clothing. In stark contrast, the Seoulites were rugged up to the nines in their coats and jackets.

However, despite the cool, my lonely battle with insomnia raged on. Nikki and I spent the days exploring, which distracted me and made the itch a distant memory. The nights,

Chapter 3: The Last Leg in Malaysia

however, were silent and long. With nothing to distract me, the itch seemed worse than ever. The only respite I had was an exhausted slumber, brought about by fresh air and our long, daily walking tours.

We returned to Malaysia the day prior to my appointment with the dermatologist. After bidding Nikki farewell (she was off to the Philippines to continue her travel journey), I made a repeat visit to the dermatologist's office. I was looking forward to my consultation with him because the combination of topical steroids, oral antihistamines and religious moisturising was displaying no results. The only thing that marginally reduced the rash was a steroidal cream that I'd 'borrowed' from Nikki; she had a prescription for a stronger dose than the one I was prescribed in her possession when she visited. However, by the time I returned to the dermatologist for my follow-up appointment, even the potent steroid she loaned me was no longer working. My rash was worse and itchier than ever.

I showed up at the medical centre only to be bitterly disappointed. I was unaware at the time, but the administrator in charge of rebooking my appointment had failed to book the follow-up with the same dermatologist. I ended up in consultation with a different specialist, which dismayed me. The lack of continuity of care meant I was forced to recount the story from the beginning, even though she had written notes from the previous clinician detailing my travel history and multiple scabies treatments.

More importantly, I was disappointed by her inability to provide me with a comparative analysis of the present rash with the rash I'd had during my first visit, the very thing the previous doctor would have been able to do. I'd hoped to receive an objective opinion of whether the rash had progressed and spread.

After a few minutes of recapping my situation and showing her the patches of rash on my body, she leaned back heavily in her seat.

"It definitely doesn't look like scabies," she said confidently.

"Unfortunately, I can't say for certain what it is. It does look like eczema caused by an allergic reaction. Eczema, however, is a very broad term used to define dry, red and itchy skin, the exact condition that you're experiencing. Eczema can be caused by various triggers, and at this stage, the exact trigger that has caused your current condition is unknown. It could be the anti-scabies treatments, the heat, or even the laundry powder your parents use. Your current condition is most likely temporary and will resolve once you're back in your normal, stable environment at home in New Zealand. Until then, make sure your skin is moisturised, continue taking antihistamines and keep using the topical steroids so that the rash stays under control. I will give you a script for a stronger dose of steroids."

I sighed in resignation.

"Is there no other alternative?" I had to try. This itch was driving me up the wall.

"Unfortunately not. I'm prescribing you all the possible solutions already. Time is your best friend at the moment," she responded.

Chapter 3: The Last Leg in Malaysia

I guess I just have to ride this out.

I thanked her for her time, collected my prescribed medication from the nearby pharmacy and left the medical centre.

End of October 2019

Almost three months had passed since we got to Malaysia. Our time was drawing to an end, with our flights back home on the night of the 22nd. I was itching (pun intended) to go home. As much as I'd enjoyed the time with my family, my parents' home and Malaysia no longer felt like home. The trip had served its purpose: I had seen Granny for the last time, bid her farewell, and the children and I had spent quality time with my parents. I was also missing my husband terribly (Cue: Awwwww. I love my man!).

On the day of our departure, I packed our suitcases, loading them with the many purchases and gifts that we had acquired throughout our stay. After countless hugs and kisses, the children and I walked through the immigration booth, waving until my parents were completely out of sight. We proceeded to replay the flight routine, only in reverse. I was more experienced travelling with toddlers this time around and took things in my stride. The return trip was also a tad easier because Holly was three months older and could now walk further distances on her own.

We arrived home on a wintry evening. We were back! The children and I were thrilled to see Rod waiting expectantly for us at the arrival gate. We had been separated for 90 days, a long time to be apart from immediate family.[9] I teared up at the sight of my husband's face in the flesh and not via video for the first time in months. The kids ran up to him; they had missed their father as much as I had.

The weather in Dunedin was bitterly cold, but it meant that we could wear our winter coats again! Remember them? When we finally sat in the car, I heaved a mental sigh of relief. We were home, and home meant an end to the itch. Things were finally going to return to normal.

We drove home to Balclutha (a small town approximately an hour's drive from Dunedin), not realising that this would be the last international trip that any of us would take for quite a while.

And that things weren't going to be normal for a long, long time.

And that things weren't going to be normal for a long, long time.

---

[9] At the time of writing, Covid-19 has ravaged the globe and families all around the world have been separated for over a span of years rather than months. I can only sympathise with these families and their plight. Three months for me was long enough.

PART 2

NEW ZEALAND

CHAPTER 4

THE PLIGHT OF ECZEMA SUFFERERS

New Zealand is a country that has a lot to offer for people who love the great outdoors. The snow-capped mountains in winter, the glaciers, the bountiful bush walks, the lakes and rivers available for all kinds of water sports and the plentiful adrenaline-fuelled activities — bungy jumping, skydiving, rock climbing — you name it, we probably have it. The beauty of the country has led some to tout it as heaven on earth, and I would agree with that viewpoint. We even have the hobbits (a reference to *The Lord of the Rings* trilogy series), something no other country can boast about.[10] Almost everyone I know who has visited New Zealand is either in love with, or at the very least, fond of this country.

---

10 *At the time of writing, the hobbits have decided to emigrate! Amazon has just announced that it will film the second season of the Lord of the Rings series in the UK. Let's hope the little people never forget their motherland.*

Personally, I was tremendously pleased to be back after spending almost three months in Malaysia. For over 20 years of my life, Malaysia was my home. But almost a decade had passed since I moved to New Zealand, and this little isolated but beautiful island country was the one I now called home. I would always be proud and fond of the country where I was born and grew up, but on our last few visits to Malaysia, I felt like a tourist rather than a resident. Home truly is where one's heart is.

Home truly is where one's heart is.

I was also really relieved about leaving the Southeast Asian heat behind and positive my itch problems would soon end. Despite the fact that it was now spring, it was still a lot cooler than Malaysia. However, a tiny part of me was worried that the source of my itch was due to treatment-resistant scabies. We were going home to a new build that was completed in our absence (the other reason Rod couldn't travel with us to Malaysia — he had to oversee our home being built), and I didn't want to introduce any mites into our brand-new space! Not having any other option, I decided to trust in the treatment that the kids and I had but resolved to pay a visit to our local GP if my condition was unresolved in a few weeks.

Chapter 4: The Plight of Eczema Sufferers

Five days later in the local doctor's office

I didn't even last a week. I told Dr Adam about my scabies scare, showed him my rash, and described my whole-body itch. He was patient and kind as he listened to my tale intently. He examined my rash carefully but, to my dismay, echoed the sentiment I'd heard from the doctors in Malaysia. Over the next few months, I'd come to resent this six-letter word: eczema.

"Is there anything you can give me to reduce the itch?" I asked helplessly. This persistent itch was starting to interrupt my daily activities. I desperately needed things to go back to normal, especially now that we were back into our day-to-day work routine. My parents weren't around to help me pick up the slack anymore.

Dr Adam surveyed the assorted tubes of steroidal creams, tubs of emollients and various antihistamine pills that I'd brought along to the appointment — all the medication prescribed to me in Malaysia. I wanted to be sure that I was on the right medication in line with New Zealand's health advice for eczema, especially because I was aware that different countries allowed different forms or brands of medication and authorised different drug concentrations for various reasons specific to the location.

"I can prescribe more antihistamines as you look like you're running out, but you're already doing all the right things," he said.

I had never felt so sorry for eczema sufferers. Growing up, I had a few friends who suffered from chronic skin problems. I remember being sympathetic and, at the same time, unintentionally dismissive. In theory, eczema is caused by dry skin, a condition that is easily resolved by consistent moisturising. Prior to this period, I wholeheartedly believed it was a simple condition with a simple solution. It was just dry skin; how bad could it be? Put some moisturiser on it; problem solved! Yet here I was in this predicament, where moisturising was doing nothing to alleviate my symptoms. It was, however, still the primary advice the doctor had for me.

"Make sure you keep moisturising. What you can also do is try to identify the source of irritation: perhaps you've developed an allergy to a certain type of material or food. If you have recently changed your habits or tried something new, perhaps try an alternative for a couple of weeks and see if your itch subsides," he continued.

Having to test and experiment to discover the possible cause of my condition seemed like an impossible task. It would take weeks, if not months, to work through eliminating different foods from my diet or possible irritants from my daily life. In order to determine the root of the problem, Dr Adam recommended eliminating only one possible irritant at a time to avoid confusion. The seven-to-fourteen-day period was recommended because results are visible only once the source of irritation has been completely eradicated from the body. However, as the order of the substances I decided to test would be based on random luck, the testing period could drag on for a long time — especially if one's luck was terrible, and the actual irritant was one of the latter items tested.

I couldn't see the finish line, and it was driving me to despair.

Chapter 4 : The Plight of Eczema Sufferers

Dr Adam also concurred with the skin reaction diagnosis that the Malaysian dermatologists had given me.

"You mentioned going through a few rounds of anti-scabies treatment…?"

"Yes, with at least two applications for each round. I know they can irritate the skin, but surely not for this long after the last treatment?" I questioned.

"It's possible that the multiple treatments have stripped your skin of all its natural oils and moisture. This could be why your itch is lasting this long. It's more than just acute irritation," he responded. "Your children are young; their skin is more supple and regenerates quicker than yours. This could explain why you're affected but not them."

That made complete sense. My youthfulness (or lack thereof) was not doing me any favours medically.

Dr Adam looked thoughtful as he tapped the lid of the large jar of emollient with his index finger. "This aqueous cream prescription you have here can double as a soap substitute. It may pay to avoid store-bought soaps and body washes for the time being, as there could be chemicals in their formula that can further strip your skin of its natural moisture. Using this during your shower instead should add a layer of protection to your skin and prevent it from drying out."

I nodded, mentally taking notes. I was open to trying anything as long as it proved helpful.

"Lastly, apply this on any particularly itchy patches that surface," he said, picking up the tube of topical steroid. "Use this only as a last resort as steroids can thin the skin and are unsuitable for the long run."

After the consultation, I walked out of his office, reassured that I was doing all the right things. Dr Adam could think of nothing new to add to my medication or my moisturising regime. I was convinced that it was only a matter of time and determined not to let eczema get the better of me or my lifestyle.

However, this eczema episode was stubborn and determined to stay. After two and a half weeks, I found myself booking in another appointment with Dr Adam, requesting further tests and solutions. Neither the itch nor the rash was abating. This follow-up visit turned out to be the first of numerous blood tests and referral letters to the dermatology department in Dunedin. Little did I know then, but Dr Adam and I were going to have six consultations in total over the course of the next two months: three of them in person and three over the phone.

Every consultation after the first two felt like a futile repetition. Each time, he asked me about possible changes in my routine I might have forgotten about that could be the cause of adverse reactions. I repeatedly told Dr Adam that nothing had changed, apart from us being in a new home. Unless I had suddenly developed an allergic response to a certain food or our laundry powder, there was nothing I could think of that would cause this extent of itching. I questioned the wisdom of scheduling appointments that were producing no real results, but my resolve not to pay the doctor a visit would falter each night when the itch reared its ugly head.

On one occasion, I sought another doctor's advice. After having to repeat my whole history only to receive the same

Chapter 4 : The Plight of Eczema Sufferers

diagnosis and arrive back at square one, I resolved to only consult with Dr Adam from then onwards. At least he had my history and was able to pick up from where we last left off.

Fortunately, Dr Adam was patient and resourceful. He would suggest at least one different approach or medical test each time we had a consult, which made me feel as if we were moving towards a resolution regardless of my unchanging condition.

There was nothing to worry about. This was the repeated conclusion drawn from the numerous tests and consultations.

Despite the mounting costs of doctor visits and repeat prescriptions, nothing helped. The hundreds of dollars I spent on medical bills during this period — general practices are considered private businesses in New Zealand and are distinct but not completely separate from public healthcare — spoke volumes about my predicament. I was exhausted and baffled. The lack of other symptoms such as fevers, nausea or night sweats pointed to the fact that this was just a simple case of eczema and nothing sinister. The numerous blood tests ordered by Dr Adam all came back with relatively normal results. My C-reactive protein and iron levels were grossly elevated, but I was told that these results were consistent with inflammatory episodes of eczema.

There was nothing to worry about. This was the repeated conclusion drawn from the numerous tests and consultations.

They couldn't have been more wrong.

They couldn't have been more wrong.

Mid-November 2019

Time passed, and things got progressively worse. I have to confess that I cannot remember the exact progression of events but have highlighted the ones that stand out due to the weight of their discomfort and the extent of their abnormality. I vividly recall my skin being so sensitive that I couldn't lie on the cotton sheets on our bed. I physically couldn't bear the way they felt on my skin. I tossed and turned every night, which in turn interrupted Rod's sleep and alertness during the day. After several days of this, I decided that it was prudent for me to sleep on the couch in the lounge to prevent further disrupting his rest. Since cotton sheets were aggravating my condition, I slept on and under soft fleece.

I also couldn't bring myself to wear certain clothing anymore. Material that didn't feel silky against the skin proved unbearable. My wardrobe went through a gradual but evident overhaul, with jeans, woollens, snug-fitting outfits, and even standard wired brassieres relegated to the back. I

Chapter 4 : The Plight of Eczema Sufferers

started living in seamless undergarments, sports tops and pants; clothing made out of lightweight and thin material that was silky to the touch.

Along with the wardrobe transition, my methods of coping with the itch reached unusual proportions. My fingernails, which had been the primary tool for dealing with the problem, were starting to fail at providing me with relief. To my physical detriment, I resorted to innovative measures of scratching that were incredibly harsh on the skin.

I started using a metal back scratcher on my legs and feet.

If you don't have a back scratcher, you're missing out. Granny had one of these — another thing I remember her fondly for. Hers was wooden with blunt fork-like 'fingers' on one end. These instruments are used to self-scratch when you have an itch on your back that you can't reach. Mine was a modern version: it was metal and was collapsible to the length of a pen. I had purchased one a few years back, not for any particular reason, but just one of those things you have (not unlike a fly swatter — an instrument that you only pull out when the occasion calls for it).

For the next few weeks, my back scratcher lived close to me and was a constant companion on the side table next to the couch I slept on. My reliance on this instrument grew with time. The blunt metal fingers dug cruelly into my skin, but I couldn't stop because it was the only thing that provided any relief. I only realised how ruthless I was when my tool snapped in two after several weeks of continual use. I cried, not because I had broken my scratcher, but because I had no respite while awaiting its replacement. To ensure I didn't find myself in the same situation again, I purchased three new ones, which to my relief, arrived promptly. Despite my rational brain and my husband telling me that my continual scratching was making things worse, the itch sensations were so deep and so intense that the only course of action was to apply increasing amounts of pressure to the scratching.

Another part of my body, besides my legs and feet, that caused a lot of anguish during this time was my back. My whole back itched terribly, and even my trusty metal back scratcher was inadequate for this broad surface. It was ironic, considering that's what back scratchers were designed for. To deal with my back, I pulled out the big guns — I acquired an acupressure spike mat.

The acupressure mat is touted as an ancient secret for the modern world. A self-care aid based on the Indian bed of nails, the numerous plastic pointy spikes on the mat, which aren't sharp enough to draw blood, work their magic by digging into pressure points on the body. My purchase of this mat came with an instructional manual depicting several men and women lying serenely atop the mat with their eyes closed and gentle smiles on their faces. The most popular and advised method of using this mat was to lie on the plastic spikes for approximately 20 minutes prior to bedtime. Routine use of the mat is said to release muscle tension and promote restful sleep. First-time users were advised to start out with a thin layer of clothing between the skin and the mat to allow the skin to adjust to the spikes.

Chapter 4 : The Plight of Eczema Sufferers

My experience with the acupressure mat was the complete opposite of the illustrations painted in the manual. The most accurate depiction of my usage is that of a cat rubbing itself against a scratch pole. It became a habit to lie on my mat every night and wriggle around while pushing back against the mat as hard as I could. The sensations produced by the friction between the spikes and my skin were deeply satisfying but, at the same time, physically damaging.

Rod reprimanded me repeatedly for the way I used the mat but could only watch as I proceeded to tear my back open with my vicious actions. Sure enough, the intense scraping between my back and the plastic spikes soon broke through my skin. I developed numerous trails of wounds and scab tissue along my back, evidence of repeated injury and repairing skin. Tragically, the damage was occurring faster than the healing. Despite knowledge and evidence of these injuries, nothing could deter me from reaching for the mat when nighttime arrived. The itch was so overwhelming that nothing else mattered apart from scratching.

Nothing.

Unfortunately for me, a side effect of consistent, vigorous scratching is calluses. These are thick, hardened layers of skin that the body develops to protect itself against friction and/or pressure. They generally develop on the extremities such as the heels or balls of the feet (caused by ill-fitting shoes) or on the palms of hands (due to constant use of certain instruments). The constant scratching to which I subjected my feet produced a callus of unusual proportions. The skin over both my feet grew thick and tough; it was as if they had a leather-like covering. This caused things to spiral further downhill. The tougher my skin got, the harder I had to scratch to alleviate the itch, and my skin became even tougher.

There seemed to be no end in sight. So, I continued scratching and prayed that the referral to the dermatologist would be approved sooner rather than later.

The medical referral system in New Zealand, on paper, is an effective and efficient process that prioritises patients based on their needs. This filters patients according to urgency, enabling those with pressing concerns to access more immediate care, an important consideration due to the severe shortage of specialists. This critical shortfall is caused by the increased emigration of qualified doctors to other countries and the high barrier to professional licensing for foreign-trained doctors. To avoid even further delays and increasing wait times, only cases that are deemed serious enough to require specialist attention are accepted for specialist care. All other patients are returned to the GPs' care.

Although the system was theoretically sound, the process was tedious, time-consuming and flawed in reality. In my case, there was a certain amount of information that just couldn't be conveyed via text or images, especially since my rash was not prominent on camera. It wasn't possible to accurately communicate through written correspondence the severity of my itch, which was the bane of my existence at the time. This episode in my life has solidified my lifelong belief that the absolute gold standard of medical care has been and always will be in-person consultations.

Chapter 4 : The Plight of Eczema Sufferers

This episode in my life has solidified my lifelong belief that the absolute gold standard of medical care has been and always will be in-person consultations.

Dr Adam and I had a difficult time grappling with the strict criteria that prevented my case from being escalated to the dermatologists. Our first application was denied due to a lack of visible evidence. When we revised the referral and attached accompanying images, the referral was rejected because my rash was deemed 'not severe enough'. According to the dermatology clinic, there were insufficient grounds for a specialist appointment. I was advised to keep the rash under control using topical steroids and antihistamines, medication that I was already on. After revising the referral yet again and sending it off, Dr Adam decided that it was time to try another route. In addition to dermatology, this time he also sent a referral letter to the internal medicine department. With both referrals out of our hands, there was little to do but pray and wait. So, I prayed.

In light of the continued rejections and seemingly unanswered prayers, I decided it was time to test out alternative remedies. For over three months, I'd heeded advice from medical professionals and adhered to prescription medication to no avail. It was time to seek other options, such as natural or traditional remedies that might help. I spent several days researching eczema in a frenzy: its causes, symptoms and remedies. I read as many health articles as I could find, joined numerous eczema support groups on Facebook and poured over the suggestions and comments in these groups. I was determined to find a solution. The numerous forums I trawled were filled with success stories as well as before and after pictures.

Someone, somewhere, had a solution for me. All I had to do was find it.

By the end of my research, I was an eczema expert. I knew every fact and myth there was about eczema. I could also have started a business trading in eczema speciality goods.

Throughout my research period, I went on a shopping spree, readily purchasing any and all recommended products endorsed as successful eczema treatments. It seemed as if every single individual in the support groups had their own trusted brand of cream or moisturiser that they swore by. I wanted to be sure I left no stone unturned, so I bought them all. The shelves in our ensuite bathroom were gradually filled to the brim with various skin products. I only needed ONE successful remedy. Surely one of the many products I purchased would do the trick.

Day after day, I moisturised faithfully using a variety of emollients. The list was long: fatty cream prescribed by the Malaysian dermatologist, a thicker moisturiser specifically for feet and hands, Sorbolene (a different brand of moisturiser), a children's moisturiser that a parent swore worked for his baby, kawakawa balm, hemp seed oil balm... The list went on and on. You name it, I probably had it. I never used them all

Chapter 4: The Plight of Eczema Sufferers

at once but rotated them on a three-to-four-day basis to see which yielded improvement.

None of them worked. None.

This went on for a few more weeks. I'd been itching continually for almost five months at this point. At the end of the first week of December, I snapped. I scheduled an appointment with Dr Adam and begged him for a solution. Nothing I was doing was working. None of the suggested remedies were even remotely helping. I desperately needed a reprieve, even if it was a temporary measure. Dr Adam took pity on me and told me that there was an option, albeit one that he was very reluctant to explore unless absolutely necessary.

"I've tried anything and everything I can," I told him. "Nothing is working. I could really use a break. I can't sleep or function properly." I looked at him pleadingly.

Dr Adam nodded understandingly. He had seen me multiple times in a relatively short span of time, so he knew that the itch was causing me extreme discomfort.

"I'll prescribe you a course of prednisone. It's not a long-term solution because extended use of oral steroids causes the adrenal glands in the body to decrease its natural production of cortisol. An abrupt halt of prednisone administration can result in withdrawal symptoms, such as fatigue, joint pain, loss of appetite and light-headedness. We'll have to wean you off gradually over time to allow your cortisol levels to return to normal," he said while typing out some notes and a prescription for me. "Steroids are notorious for side effects like weight gain, changes in mood and energy levels, but it will suppress the inflammatory response and hopefully alleviate the itch."

He printed out the prescription, signed it with a flourish and handed it to me with a warning. "Oral steroids are highly discouraged and only used as a last resort. If you can cope using other methods, those would be preferable. I've prescribed you a tapering dose over a period of three weeks, so be sure to follow the recommended regime."

I thanked him profusely and left his office, immensely grateful. Here was a solution to my problems! However, being aware of the downsides of oral steroids, I resolved not to fill in the script unless I absolutely needed to.

A mere 24 hours later, I caved.

I could hear Jesus admonishing me just as He did His disciples over 2000 years ago. After so many months of itching, my spirit was willing, but my flesh was weak.[11] In hindsight, filling the script was the wrong thing to do, just as it was a mistake for the disciples to fall asleep. However, I was blinded by my physical need.

As it turned out, prednisone was MAGIC.

In just two days, my rash cleared, and the itch subsided to a manageable level. Within a week, I was back to sleeping in my bed instead of the couch. For the first time in months, life returned to a pre-itch normal. The scabs on my back healed and melted away as if they were never there. My reliance on

---

11 *Matt 26:41: "Watch and pray so that you will not fall into temptation. The spirit is willing, but the body is weak."*

Chapter 4 : The Plight of Eczema Sufferers

the acupressure mat and metal back scratcher lessened, and I started wearing my normal clothing again.

The course of steroids was not without side effects — I suffered from insomnia, hot flushes, increased sweating and an increased appetite — all of which intensified over the course of the three weeks. I could see why Dr Adam had held off prescribing them. However, in the grand scheme of things, these side effects were a small price to pay for what I deemed a return to normalcy. Things were looking up, just in time for the Christmas and New Year period. I was looking forward to some relaxing time with my family now that my physical, emotional and mental state was more stable. This agonising period in life was over, and 2020 was going to be a year of new and happy beginnings — one that was itch and eczema free!

Or so I thought.

CHAPTER 5

ALTERNATING BETWEEN JOB AND JOB'S FRIENDS

I didn't know it at the time, but the first two months of 2020 were the darkest period of my life; physically, mentally, emotionally and spiritually. As I look back now, it's illuminating to discover that the lowest point in my life was not the cancer battle itself. Instead, it was the months leading up to the actual diagnosis. During this period, I came to know myself and my God intimately.

I want to stress that I'm not proud of the way I handled myself during this time. It pains and shames me to write these words, and I'm crying tears of both thanksgiving and repentance as I type. If you're a Jesus-follower going through a dark and trying time in your life, I hope that my honest testimony in this chapter will help steer you back to where your focus should be: on Him. If you, like me, have faltered, know that you are not alone. It may be difficult to see God's mercy and grace in light of immediate circumstances, but His grace is indeed sufficient. It's just that, as mere mortals, we can't see the forest for the trees in our moment of pain and suffering. In my case, once the fog lifted, I could see how He was working every step of the way for good. Hindsight is a wonderful thing.

The prednisone Dr Adam prescribed gave me respite for approximately four weeks. Although I wasn't completely itch-free, my symptoms subsided sufficiently for me to spend an enjoyable end of year holiday period with my family. However, the tapering dose regime meant that by the end of the third week, I was weaned off the medication. I was apprehensive the effects of the steroid would not last. Sure enough, once off the drugs, the itch and rash rebounded with a vengeance. In fact, I ended up in a worse state compared to before. I didn't think it was possible to get any itchier, but I was wrong. If I was suffering prior to prednisone, the itch after the rebound was pure agony.

However, there was a silver lining even in this situation. The intermittent and mild rash that had disappeared with the oral medication made a vicious comeback. My arms, legs and torso erupted in red, angry lesions. Finally, I had persuasive visual evidence that could be presented to the specialist department. Armed with impressive images of terrible-looking skin, Dr Adam added the fresh images to the referral and sent it to the dermatology department. We were both determined to get me a consultation with a specialist.

Chapter 5: Alternating Between Job and Job's Friends

It was during this time that my cough started getting worse. Prior to this, I only coughed occasionally. It was a matter of little inconvenience and a symptom I'd previously put down to the Malaysian haze. This same cough, which had not resolved, now became an ongoing issue. My throat itched constantly. I couldn't breathe deeply or inhale through my mouth without breaking into a coughing fit. To combat the itch in my throat, I stocked up on strong mint lozenges. After trialling several brands, I found that the ones that worked best were the sugar-free, mint-flavoured lozenges by Fisherman's Friend. The menthol in the lozenges provided cool relief, prompting me to suck on lozenges all day. I itched both internally and externally, with no relief in sight! My only respite was the few hours of sleep I managed in the wee hours of the morning. I yearned for those hours when I could escape the physical torment plaguing my body.

I grew more and more exhausted. My calm outer facade started to crack, and my mood grew from bad to worse. The first people to bear witness and suffer the brunt of those cracks were the ones closest to me. We usually hurt the people we love most, perhaps because we know they'll love us despite our shortcomings. I was a prime example of this unfortunate occurrence, something I'm determined to change in my life. The people that I love most are the people that I need to cherish most. At the time, however, my temper grew short, and my patience wore thin when I was around family.

Amy Ewald

---

*We usually hurt the people we love most,
perhaps because we know they'll love us
despite our shortcomings.*

Rod, my beloved and long-suffering husband, was the first recipient of my unpleasant behaviour. He put up with my emotional tirades and verbal outbursts with superhuman patience. In an effort to alleviate my misery, he started doing more of the household chores — an enormous and unconditionally loving feat for someone who worked ten-to-twelve-hour shifts. I thank the Lord daily for my husband. God knew exactly what He was doing when He brought Rod into my life.[12] I couldn't ask for a man better suited to me.

Lucas and Holly were great distractions when they were home. Their constant energy and activities kept me occupied. However, with the constant activity came continual requests (read: demands) that stretched my emotional and mental capacity. As a result, I was also unpleasant with the children. When they were at daycare, I busied myself working at the local pool as a lifeguard and operating my portrait photography business. When they were home, my life revolved around their wants, needs and comfort. I was trying to juggle several balls — being a wife, mother, homemaker, as well as income earner.

---

[12] *More precisely, He brought me into Rod's life. If we connect, do ask me how Rod and I met each other. It's a really good story!*

Chapter 5: Alternating Between Job and Job's Friends

With only 24 hours in a day, there was no room or time for me or my needs. The physical, mental and emotional anguish of juggling my daily tasks with insufficient sleep and unbearable physical discomfort took its toll on me. I grew short and irritable. All it took for me to blow my top was a simple matter of the kids messing up the lounge I had just cleared or not flushing the toilet.

My family were not the only ones I behaved like this with. I'm ashamed to say this, but I also lost my cool with God.

I'm ashamed to say this, but I also lost my cool with God.

I grew up in a Christian home, surrounded by a church family. Rather than fairy tales, from a young age, I was read children's Bible stories at bedtime. My biblical knowledge grew with age. Having an active youth group which organised activities such as Bible quizzes meant that I was trained to know the 'right' answers to questions and could spout suitable Bible verses for different life situations. I knew about my identity as God's child and that being His child didn't always mean that life was going to be a bed of roses. I was aware that in order to shape my character, life could and would be challenging.

Theoretically, I knew exactly how a Christian was meant to respond to trials. I even knew the exact verse to quote to anyone who needed help: James 1:2, which reads, "Consider it pure joy, my brothers, whenever you face trials of many kinds" comes to mind quite readily. However, knowledge and action are two completely different things. It is funny how I so very conveniently missed recalling what the Bible has to say about that: "Anyone, then, who knows the good he ought to do and doesn't do it, sins" (James 4:17). When push came to shove, I couldn't live out the things I'd learned and had known for years. I certainly didn't count any of my suffering as pure joy, nor could I emulate Job by blessing God's name.[13]

Instead, I alternated between vocally venting my anger at God and questioning what I did to deserve my predicament (which in all truth was probably plenty, considering I was and am an imperfect being). There were a lot of 'Why me, God?!' prayers and 'Surely I've suffered long enough, Lord?!' questions from me. In several angry prayers, I took on the role of Job's friends. I was convinced that my suffering was a direct punishment for my sins and confessed all the wrongdoings that I could remember.

Surely God would take this curse away if I repented.

In other prayers, I was Job. I'd done nothing terribly wrong that I knew of or could recall. I did, however, manage to stop

---

[13] *Job is a biblical character who maintained his spiritual piety despite losing everything he had — his children, possessions and his health. According to Job 1:21: And said: "Naked I came from my mother's womb, and naked I will depart. The Lord gave and the Lord has taken away; may the name of the Lord be praised." During this period of affliction, Job's wife advised him to curse God and die, while his friends steadfastly maintained that Job must have committed a grievous sin against God and that his sufferings were a result of his transgression.*

Chapter 5: Alternating Between Job and Job's Friends

short of taking Job's wife's advice to curse God and die,[14] and for that I am eternally thankful.

Throughout the almost six months of suffering, I uttered numerous prayers and requests. In the beginning, they were but a passing request for relief. As time passed, my prayers grew more heartfelt, emotional but also highly inconsistent. In one, I would selfishly and foolishly claim that God's grace was not sufficient for me.[15] I insisted that I needed more grace and was really angry at God for not granting me what I believed I was entitled to. Doing a complete 180, my next prayer would be filled with fear and repentance.

How dare I talk to God like that?!

I would apologise for my demands and plead for mercy. This yo-yo pattern continued for a few weeks. My judgement had clouded over, and I was blinded by my suffering. I lost sight of all the past blessings, the grace and the abundance that the Lord had blessed me with. All I could see was the present trial, which loomed larger than life. I cannot recall very many details of what was truly one of the darkest periods in my life as a follower of Christ, only that I was in extreme physical discomfort. Cold showers and ice-laden compresses were a part of my daily routine, all efforts to alleviate the never-abating itch.

---

14 *Job 2:9: His wife said to him, "Are you still holding on to your integrity? Curse God and die!"*

15 *2 Corinthians 12:9a: But he said to me, "My grace is sufficient for you, for my power is made perfect in weakness."*

Amy Ewald

My judgement had clouded over, and I was blinded by my suffering.

One particular shower incident still stands out today, one that I'll never forget for the rest of my life. I was having a scaldingly hot shower — possibly my only hot shower throughout this whole ordeal — when I broke down. With tears streaming down my face, I shouted at and questioned God. I needed an answer for the reason I was suffering! I screamed out my frustration, cried until I could cry no more, and ended up on my knees with water pouring down on me.

Why are You doing this?

Haven't I suffered enough by now?

It has been MONTHS, Lord. MONTHS!

Am I really your daughter? Do you truly love me?

I apologised to God profusely for being so dismissive about people itching or having eczema in the past. I told the Lord that I'd learned my lesson, in case He was trying to educate me and begged for deliverance.

Despite the heartfelt begging and crying, I heard nothing.

There was no bright light from heaven.

No revelation, vision or heavenly message.

Nothing but the continual cascade of hot water streaming down my body.

Chapter 5: Alternating Between Job and Job's Friends

That shower ended quite unremarkably. Strangely, however, I felt at peace. Perhaps it was because the itch was momentarily soothed by the hot water. Or because I'd cried my heart out in the shower until I was void of tears. Maybe the peace was a result of one of the most honest prayers I'd ever offered to God. I had poured my heart out and God had truly seen and heard the worst of me. I was bare and naked before Him and had nothing left to hide.

The only people who were spared my emotional tirades were my parents.

I wish I could say that I did it out of love and to spare them the emotional anguish of worrying about my situation. Truthfully though, the decision to keep them in the dark was for completely selfish reasons. My parents and I spoke to each other via video calls periodically, as it was important for Lucas and Holly to keep in contact with their grandparents. However, since we returned to New Zealand, every conversation I had with my parents was marred by their enquiries about whether the itch that plagued me in Malaysia had subsided. To circumvent their continual questioning, I blatantly lied.

I told them that my itch had resolved, and things were back to normal.

Although I had no sinister intentions when I lied, it was a disgusting act of self-preservation. In my exhaustion, I felt as if I had zero capacity to care for my parents emotionally. I already had a lot to deal with and didn't need more emotional baggage. I didn't want to bear the burden of fielding their concerned questions and well-meaning advice, knowing well that would be the case if the truth surfaced. In my mind, there was very little they could actually do to help since they were so geographically distant.

The downside of keeping my condition a secret was that I reduced our video conversations to a quick hi and bye on my part. I intentionally focused most of our calls on the children, who entertained their grandparents with silly antics and stories. If my parents noticed my purposeful distance and lack of communication, they were kind enough not to mention it.[16]

Time marched steadily on.

A few days into the new year, I received a letter from the dermatology department in Dunedin officially declining my referral request. They were not going to see me, photo evidence or not. I called my health practice to convey the message to Dr Adam, who was prompt to return my call.

"You have an appointment to meet with Dr John in a few days!" he announced triumphantly. "It's a pity dermatology won't accept our referral, but Dr John from internal medicine might be able to help. He may have another opinion or other thoughts about what we can try."

---

[16] *I've been asked what I would do if history repeated itself. Would I tell them off the bat? Or would I keep it to myself again? The honest answer: I don't know. It remains true that we are separated by geographical distance, and I wouldn't want them worrying from afar. I believe that every situation is unique and by extension, every response. I hope I never have to find out.*

Chapter 5: Alternating Between Job and Job's Friends

I agreed enthusiastically. It was a relief to be making some form of progress up the chain of doctor command. Internal medicine was a speciality branch and essentially a hospital outpatient unit that could get me one step further into the health system. Before ending our conversation, I updated Dr Adam on my current situation, which prompted him to issue me a brand-new script for another course of prednisone.

"The steroids worked. It may just be a case of putting you on a slower wean to ensure there isn't a rebound," he assured me.

"Do you think I should start on this course of steroids or wait until after I've met with Dr John?"

Dr Adam paused.

"Hmm, if you can hold out until you consult with him, that would be advisable. He may be able to make a more accurate diagnosis if there are visible signs of your rash. It's only a few days away, so do your best to resist."

"I'll do my best."

It took all my willpower to hold out from filling in the prescription. Thankfully, I managed to withstand the temptation with the knowledge that the appointment was only a few days away.

Barely two weeks into January of 2020, I met with Dr John in his office. He was attentive, sympathetic and very thorough. I was questioned extensively on my medical history and carefully examined. At the end of our appointment, I was convinced that he had left no stone unturned.

He leaned forward and looked me in the eye.

"You're probably tired of hearing this, but it does look like eczema. It sounds likely that you may have a triad of conditions: asthma, eczema, and allergic rhinitis, also known as hay fever. These conditions are closely related and it's possible the abundance of pollen during this season is what's causing your allergic reactions," he explained.

"It's unfortunate that you've encountered pollen in New Zealand right after your scabies and haze episode in Malaysia. It's a case of one situation blending right into the other, causing your symptoms to drag out for an extended amount of time."

"Is there truly nothing else that can be done?" I inquired desperately.

He shook his head sadly. "The best thing to do is let it run its course. Keep moisturising and take the antihistamines on an as-needed basis. I will prescribe an antihistamine-based nasal spray that may relieve the irritation in your nasal cavity and suppress the cough. Let's try that for a few weeks to see if it helps."

First it was haze and eczema. Now it was asthma and hay fever. All conditions that doctors could do nothing about. Seriously?!

This was getting ridiculous.

His expression turned sombre.

Chapter 5: Alternating Between Job and Job's Friends

"I'd strongly advise against a second course of prednisone. A major side effect of oral steroids is a decreased ability of your body to deposit bone material, and the long-lasting effects of this reduction can be devastating. Osteoporosis is a significant worry, particularly with your gender and heritage," he cautioned, referring to the fact that Asians are at a higher risk of developing osteoporosis.

My heart sank at his words. I wasn't entirely sure what I was expecting Dr John to say that Dr Adam hadn't, but I'd had a tiny glimmer of hope prior to the appointment. Hope for a different diagnosis and different treatment. Any alternative he could think of would have been better than the cocktail of therapies I was already on, particularly because nothing was working. This appointment had, however, dashed all my hopes, and even worse, robbed me of the one and only magical remedy that did work — the little round pink steroid pills.

I don't know for sure how I made it through the first two months of 2020. The human body is more resilient than what we give it credit for, and life continued despite my physical distress. To this day, I wonder how I managed to carry on as per normal, but the reality was that I had no choice. Officially, there was nothing wrong with me. Off the record, everything was wrong, and I was a total wreck.

Before January was over, I was on a myriad of topical and oral medications. It wouldn't have been inappropriate for a stranger to assume I had a drug dependency. I'd lost some weight, my eyes had dark circles under them, and my body bore injury marks from excessive scratching. I was unravelling. My only saving grace at this time was yet another, albeit less magical pill that I'd managed to convince Dr Adam to prescribe in place of steroids: the humble sleeping pill.

Dr Adam made it clear that he was very hesitant to prescribe these to me, but even he felt like things were getting out of hand. He was utterly perplexed by my condition. Biologically, things were normal. The repeated blood tests I had showed nothing sinister. My C-reactive protein levels were now over the roof compared to earlier tests (mine were consistently over 65 compared to the standard level of <5 mg/L), my platelet levels were high and haemoglobin levels were low — but these results were all consistent with chronic eczema inflammation. Because Dr Adam had no other suggestions or solutions for me, he reluctantly issued me a script for sleeping pills after we had an in-depth discussion about the suitable doses, tolerance and the danger of overdosing.

After almost six months of anguish, something inside of me broke. Something was terribly wrong with me, but no one had any idea what it was. My medical team was clueless, as was I. God, whom I had wept to continually for answers, remained silent.

God, whom I had wept to continually for answers, remained silent.

Chapter 5: Alternating Between Job and Job's Friends

Rod came home from work one day to find me sitting curled up in the bathtub, sobbing silently. I was testing out yet another suggested cure that I have to thank the eczema support group on Facebook for — a tepid oatmeal bath — while Lucas and Holly watched TV. Thirty minutes prior, I had caved and called him at work, pleading with him to come home. He was originally scheduled to work till 8 pm (past the kids' bedtime), which meant that I had to prepare dinner, clean the kitchen, shower the kids and do the bedtime routine all by myself. The prospect of having to care for the children's needs in my condition was crippling. I was mentally and physically depleted and had reached the end of my tether.

So, I cried to my husband for help. Rod knew how badly I was affected on a physical level, but I don't think he truly comprehended the enormity of the demons that I had to wrestle with every night. Witnessing the soaking mess in the bathtub that day gave him a deeper understanding of just how severely this ordeal was affecting me. Being the amazing man he is, he took the next few days off to care for the children while I tried to get some rest and put my needs first. He also had a grand idea: we needed to go away on a family holiday. We had not spent any quality time with each other since the children and I returned from Malaysia. He had some annual leave saved up, and it was time to cash that in and do something fun together. A brief change in environment would do us all some good!

After a lengthy discussion while I stewed in the tepid oatmeal bath (which by the way, was an uncomfortable, cold and unfruitful endeavour), we agreed that he would apply for annual leave and take a whole month off work beginning at the end of February. Subject to his leave approval, we would spend a week in Christchurch and Wanaka for a brief holiday and three weeks at home with him in charge domestically. All I had to do was try to get as much sleep as I could.

At Rod's insistence, I also booked another appointment to see Dr John. My husband was right: I needed a simpler medication regime. At that moment, I was on so many different types of oral and topical medication that were essentially doing nothing. Dr John agreed and drastically reduced my medication. He simplified my therapy by replacing my numerous pills with just one: doxepin, a drug used to treat hives, depression, anxiety and insomnia. Unfortunately, doxepin is an uncommon therapy that is not publicly subsidised by the health system.

This chronic issue was not only tiresome, but it was also proving to be extremely expensive. I'd had numerous medical appointments, prescriptions, and suggested remedies in the past six months, all of which added up to a substantial amount of money.

Despite the increased financial burden, my attention was now directed to the holiday that we had planned. In an effort to distract me, Rod gave me a fun assignment: I was in charge of organising our activities in both Christchurch and Wanaka. Although the trip wasn't for a few weeks yet, the distraction worked. I had something to look forward to and plan for. I was also excited as I was looking forward to visiting these two cities I had not been to before. The prospect of a new start after the holiday kept me going.

Until we hit a bump in the road that changed all our plans.

CHAPTER 6

THE BUMP IN THE ROAD

Finding a lump on any part of your body will make you pause. The visible bump that I discovered didn't just give me reason to pause, it brought all my life plans to a screeching halt. I am, however, forever humbled and eternally grateful that my six-month hiatus from life occurred at the same time as the world's (due to Covid). It was as if God held the sun still for me while I fought my battle, just as He did for Joshua (Chapter 10 in the book of Joshua records an event whereby God delayed the setting of the sun for a day during a battle between the Amorites and the Israelites).[17]

---

17 *Joshua 10:12-13:*
[12] On the day the Lord gave the Amorites over to Israel, Joshua said to the Lord in the presence of Israel:
"O sun, stand still over Gibeon,
O moon, over the Valley of Aijalon."
[13] So the sun stood still,
and the moon stopped,
till the nation avenged itself on its enemies,
as it is written in the Book of Jashar.
The sun stopped in the middle of the sky and delayed going down about a full day.

Recalling this gives me goosebumps till today. For now, let's get on with the story.

7th of February 2020. Friday night

I was having a cool shower after putting the kids to bed. Rod was in the kitchen cleaning up the mess (read: the kids' mess) from our evening meal. It was while washing my neck that my left hand discovered something foreign. There was a small, but prominent lump right above my right collarbone.

That's strange. Was this present yesterday?

I reached for the other side of my neck.

Nope, nothing on that side.

I moved my hand back to the lump on the right.

Yup, definitely a bump that's not on the other side. What is it?

I quickly finished my shower, turned the water off and towelled myself dry. I stood in front of the mirror, peering intently to examine my newfound discovery. It felt semi-solid to the touch. Not too soft, not too hard. Had it been the description of the perfect resting place, Goldilocks would have been so happy.

It's definitely noticeable. I wonder why I haven't noticed it before today.

I dressed quickly and went to the lounge to show Rod my lump.

Chapter 6: The Bump in the Road

"I can definitely see it. It isn't obvious, though. I wouldn't have noticed if you hadn't mentioned it. Does it hurt?" he asked, applying gentle pressure to the bump.

"No, not at all. Do you think it could be my lymph nodes swelling up? Maybe the allergies cause an immune response…?"

"Could be." Rod looked thoughtful. "I think you should call your doctor on Monday. It won't hurt to get it checked. Probably a good idea with all that's going on," he advised.

I nodded. "I'll book an appointment first thing Monday morning."

Monday came along, and I found myself in Dr Adam's office yet again. By this time, he was not at all surprised to see me considering I was now a regular visitor. He was, however, surprised that I was not there because of the itch.

"It looks like swollen lymph nodes. I wouldn't worry about it," he said, gently probing at my neck with his fingers. "They're probably swelling as a result of the hay fever. You've been suffering the effects of the allergies for a long time, so it was only a matter of time before your immune system reacted."

He rolled his chair back and looked at me.

"I will, however, refer you to the radiology department for an ultrasound. A lump is still a lump, and it's better to get it medically checked, considering your current circumstances."

He swivelled his chair to face his computer screen and tapped rapidly at his keyboard. A few seconds later, he printed out a referral note and handed it to me.

"Book an appointment with Pacific Radiology. Their reception is just around the corner." He gestured to the door with his hands. "They are pretty busy at the moment, so your appointment probably won't be for a few weeks. In the meantime, keep an eye on the lump. If it recedes and things go back to normal prior to your appointment date, just call up and cancel your appointment."

I thanked him and left his office for the radiology department.

"Is there nothing sooner?" I asked the booking administrator.

She had just offered me an appointment on the 6th of April, a full eight weeks away.

I am very blessed to be eligible for publicly funded, heavily subsidised health care services in New Zealand. However, due to demand outstripping resources — as is usual in the health sector — my case, which seemed in theory to be a simple issue of enlarged lymph nodes, put me at the very bottom of the urgency scale.

"If you'd like to book a private appointment, we have an opening next week on the 19th…?" she trailed off inquiringly.

Of course.

Chapter 6: The Bump in the Road

I'd forgotten that money was the VIP pass. There was indeed a way to ascend the urgency scale, and that was by paying for the privilege. Upon full payment for the cost of the procedure, one would be assigned to the private health care roll, which is oftentimes less subscribed to than the public one for obvious reasons.

I paused for a fraction of a second.

"If I book in the one for April but decide to come in sooner, will I be able to change my booking over the phone?"

An earlier appointment was important, but I wanted to check in with Rod before committing to a costly procedure.

"Sure, just give us a ring on this number," she replied, her index finger pointing to the number inscribed on the appointment card she slid towards me.

"Awesome, thank you for your help!" I took the card, shoved it in my pocket and headed back to the car.

The very first thing I did once I was seated was to pull out my phone and consult with Dr Google. I trusted my doctor, but he had obviously decided that this lump was significant enough to refer me for an ultrasound. He wouldn't have done that if he was 100 per cent sure it was just swollen lymph nodes, so I wanted to explore the other possibilities. I typed 'itchy skin neck lump' into the search bar and tapped enter. The results loaded within milliseconds, and I stared at the first search result at the top of the page, my heart pounding in my ears.

The very first link read: Symptoms of lymphoma.[18]

---

18 *https://lymphoma-action.org.uk/symptoms-of-lymphoma*

The rest of the day passed by slowly. I needed to have a discussion with my husband, but the presence of young children at home is the best deterrent for any form of serious conversation. That night, after the kids had gone to bed, I sat down with Rod. I told him about my appointment with Dr Adam, the ultrasound referral and appointment in April, and my Google search results. I mentioned I was considering paying for the ultrasound, which would get me seen the following week. He listened intently, not interrupting until I was finished.

"Dr Adam thinks it's nothing serious?" he asked.

"Yeah." I sighed. "What do you think, hun? Should we fork out $250 for an ultrasound for something that may end up being nothing? It's a decent sum to spend on nothing, and it's money that should be used on our home instead."

Although our newly built home was 95 per cent finished, there were loose ends and odd jobs (such as applying silicone to fill in gaps) that needed completing. Each task, although small and inexpensive on its own compared to the overall project, added up to generate an impressive sum that was consuming a healthy chunk of our financial resources. In addition, the unexpected but necessary medical costs that I'd been incurring were creating a substantial dent in our savings. I wasn't sure if I could justify spending another $250 to expedite an unnecessary scan.

Was it unnecessary? We were both unsure.

Chapter 6: The Bump in the Road

Rod looked thoughtful while he considered the options. I looked down at my phone, which displayed the results I'd looked up that same afternoon. I scrolled through, my eyes scanning the first page. It wasn't just the first link. The whole first (and even second) page was filled with various lymphoma references. I was torn. On the one hand, a lymphoma diagnosis made sense. It would explain the chronic cough and itch and why the medication wasn't working. On the other hand, I was doubtful. I'd looked through the lymphoma links prior to my conversation with Rod and read about the most common symptoms — fever, fatigue, night sweats — all of which I had not experienced. A lymphoma diagnosis was plausible but, in my mind, unlikely.

"Just book it in, love," he said after a long pause.

"You think so?"

"Yup, let's do it. It probably isn't lymphoma, but it's a major symptom that may lead to a firmer diagnosis. This might give us answers to your itch. You've been suffering for months, so let's not put it off any longer than necessary."

I nodded in agreement. "You're right. I'll call them first thing tomorrow."

"I wouldn't worry too much about it, though," he continued. "Dr Adam did say that it's probably nothing, so let's not lose sleep over it until the ultrasound results are out."

I nodded, reassured.

The following week

"Amy Ewald?" the sonographer on duty called for me at the entrance to the imaging room. I stood up and walked into the room. She closed the door behind me, leaving us both in the dark, the only light in the small space emanating from the various computer screens present.

The sonographer was friendly and assuring.

"I see you're here for a neck scan due to a lump?" she asked, peering down at my notes.

I nodded. "Is that normal? Do you see these quite a bit?"

"We see lumps at the weirdest places for the strangest reasons on a daily basis. A lot of them are nothing to worry about and are caused by lymphatic drainage issues," she said with a smile.

She gestured for me to lie atop a hard, narrow bed and turn my head to the side. I gingerly climbed onto the bed and angled my head towards the wall while she sat on an elevated chair next to me and picked up the ultrasound wand.

"Have you had an infection recently?" she asked, squirting a generous amount of lubricant on the tip of the wand.

I told her about my eczema/hay fever issues. "My doctor said it could just be the lymph nodes swelling up," I concluded.

"It could be. Let's have a look, shall we? This might be a bit cold," she warned.

I kept my silence while she got on with her task. For several long minutes, she imaged various regions of my right neck area with the wand. The room was completely silent

Chapter 6: The Bump in the Road

apart from the whirring of the machinery and the tapping of keys on the keyboard as she recorded the images on the screen.

She broke the silence first.

"There's definitely something here. I can't seem to tell what it is, but the radiologist might be able to," she said, peering at her computer screen. "Can you please turn your head the other way so I can do the other side of your neck?"

"Are we doing both sides?" I asked, rotating to face the other direction. "I only have a lump on the right."

"We often image both sides of the same body part so that we have something to compare it to. Different people can have different anatomies and slightly different sizes, so a comparison between the normal and abnormal region of the same individual gives us a more accurate representation of what's normal and what's not."

That made sense.

She began performing the same procedure on the left side of my neck. After several more minutes, we were done. I gratefully accepted the wipes she handed me and cleaned the lubricant off my neck while she turned the lights on.

"That wasn't too bad," I remarked with a small smile, pushing myself up to a sitting position on the bed. "Do you know when I can expect the results?"

"You should know within the next day or so," she replied. "I'll send your images to the radiologist right away. He'll interpret them and send the results to your GP, who will then be in touch."

"Awesome, thank you for your help!"

I tossed the used wipes into a nearby trash can, picked up my bag and left the room. I paid for the scan and left the building, mentally calculating and adjusting our budget to ensure we had sufficient resources to last us till our next payday.

It turned out, however, that God was going to provide for my needs (as He always does) as long as I was prepared to do the work.

I got home, turned my computer on and logged into my business email account. The first email was from an acquaintance inquiring about a headshot for her employee. Picking up my phone, I called her to determine the nature of the images she required. By the end of our conversation, I'd secured the job at almost the same amount of money I'd just spent on the ultrasound. Talk about perfect timing.

Was it coincidence or provision?

A lot of the time, patients are frustrated when they don't hear back from their doctor after a certain procedure or test. Personally, I've not been exempt from such feelings in the past. Although health service providers could do better in communicating with their patients, it's common knowledge that the workload in these departments is extremely high. Every precious second counts and they have little time to spare reassuring patients that everything is well. I have long

Chapter 6: The Bump in the Road

learned that the old idiom 'no news is good news' rings true where the public health system is concerned.

> *I have long learned that the old idiom 'no news is good news' rings true where the public health system is concerned.*

So, when Dr Adam rang me that very same afternoon, I instinctively knew that something was wrong. Same day results usually meant bad news.

"We don't know what it is," he said.

That seemed to be the main theme of this nightmare I was in.

"Okay...?" I responded, hoping for more information.

"The ultrasound was insufficient to determine the nature of the collection that is causing the lump."

"The collection?" I echoed inquiringly.

"It's the exact term used in the ultrasound report. The radiologist couldn't interpret it based on the ultrasound alone. According to him, it looks like an abnormal collection of fluid that is sufficiently concerning to warrant further testing. He recommended an urgent review by a specialist."

Whoa.

I was taken aback. Just a few hours ago, I was under the impression that it was nothing. An urgent specialist review didn't sound like nothing to me. This was a lot to take in.

"I've spoken to a specialist at the ENT (Ear, Nose and Throat) department in Dunedin. He has an appointment available for you on Friday morning. Would that suit you?" Dr Adam asked.

Hold up. Dr Adam had already arranged it?

I did some mental calculations. My scan was a mere four hours ago. And Friday was only two days away.

This had to be serious for things to move this quickly.

I wasn't going to turn down the appointment. Even if my schedule was packed, I was going to reschedule everything to make it. Here was an opportunity to finally get a firm diagnosis, however scary that might be.

"Sure. What time and where?"

I scribbled down the directions and information Dr Adam gave me onto a notepad. My mind was racing with the multiple possibilities and severity of my condition that I barely registered everything he was saying to me. I wrote on autopilot, my ears sending direct information to my hands without even thinking. After he'd given me the details, I thanked him and hesitated before addressing the elephant in the room.

Saying it would make it more real, but I had to know.

"Is it lymphoma?" I blurted out.

Dr Adam paused for half a second before responding.

"I can't say for sure and don't want to give you inaccurate information. At this stage, it's a lump that isn't normal. We're going to require further testing to determine the diagnosis.

Chapter 6: The Bump in the Road

Lymphoma is a possibility, yes, but I wouldn't worry about it incessantly before we get a definite diagnosis."

It had to be lymphoma. I just knew it.

The symptoms matched. Everything fit into place. A lymphoma diagnosis would explain the persistent itch and rash. There was a small part of me, however, that held onto the hope that it was not. After all, itching was one of the rarer symptoms.

Immediately after my conversation with Dr Adam, I rang Rod at work.

"Friday, you say?" he asked.

"Yup. 11:30 am."

"I'll be there," my husband said without hesitation. "I'll take an hour or so off work and go with you."

We spoke a little longer before hanging up. Rod, just like Dr Adam, was of the opinion we should not lose any sleep over an uncertain diagnosis. We also decided that it wasn't a suitable time to tell my parents.

Not until things were certain.

I didn't worry. Truly, I didn't. I lost no sleep over my yet-to-be-certain diagnosis. What I was, however, was information-driven. As I come from a scientific background and education, it was impossible not to research lymphoma. So, I spent the rest of the day and Thursday researching cancer and lymphoma.

Cancer is one of life's many mysteries. Many people are touched by it in one way or the other. Most people, at some point in their lives, either experience it directly themselves or are impacted indirectly through family, friends or acquaintances. I would go as far as stating that at some point, everyone's life is touched by the C-word, and it is never pleasant. In my case, it was my paternal grandfather who passed away due to cancer when I was young. I also knew of several members in our church family who had or were still suffering from cancer.

However, despite my familiarity with cancer, it remained very removed from my life. I, for one, had definitely not considered the possibility of having to battle cancer. The C-word was always something that affected someone else. The other person. My role was to support, assist and pray for them. Never did I think it would strike so close to home. It was at that point I realised how little I knew about lymphoma. I strived to learn everything I could about it. If knowledge was power, I was going to ensure I was well-equipped.

The other thing I did was pray. I don't remember my exact prayers or requests, save one: a plea for peace.

I don't remember my exact prayers or requests, save one: a plea for peace.

A cancer diagnosis, while terrifying, was the answer to all my questions and symptoms. It would, in a strange way, lift a

Chapter 6: The Bump in the Road

weight off my shoulders. I had been experiencing symptoms for months, and the doctors had been treating the symptoms as conditions. Having a single, definitive diagnosis was, in my opinion, an improvement over having several unexplainable conditions. At the same time, I was conflicted.

Of all things, did it have to be cancer? I'd take eczema over cancer any day!

Friday dawned.

I drove into Dunedin, and Rod met me at the hospital entrance ten minutes prior to our appointment time.

We met with two doctors at the ENT department. I answered a long list of routine questions, during which Dr Sam highlighted another symptom that I had not noticed.

Unexplained significant weight loss.

I knew I'd lost some weight due to the lack of sleep and persistent itch, but I didn't think it was anything remarkable. The scale I stood on in the doctor's office told another story. I had lost close to six kilograms (the equivalent of just over thirteen pounds) in six weeks without changing my exercise routine or my diet. That was just over ten per cent of my body weight in what was a short period of time.

"I suppose even cancer has its perks," I remarked jokingly to Rod, already working on the presumption that it was cancer.

Both Dr Sam and Dr Mike said that the absence of night sweats and fevers was a good sign. After a lengthy consultation, they both agreed that the best course of action was to conduct several biopsies — one for the nasal passage and another at the collection site, aka the bump. Tissue sampling and testing were the next steps toward a definite diagnosis.

I signed the consent forms on the spot. As far as I was concerned, the sooner the better.

Months of uncertainty had worn me down. A definite diagnosis, even if it was cancer, was welcomed.

Both biopsies proved to be extremely daunting and uncomfortable. The nasal biopsy involved inserting a pincer-like instrument up the nose and tearing off some tissue from the roof of the nasal cavity. One would think that cutting off a portion of tissue would pose less trauma compared to a vicious grab and tear. Dr Sam informed me that contrary to popular belief, cutting causes a larger trauma because human tissue has natural connections that tie them together, much like the grain you see in a piece of steak. Allowing tissue to tear according to its natural connection point allows for more natural healing.

I was given several spritzes of an unpleasant-tasting numbing spray prior to the procedure, which eliminated the pain but not the discomfort or dull throbbing that resulted. Fortunately, it only took a total of three attempts to secure sufficient tissue for testing.

After the consultation and nasal biopsy, Rod and I left for the neck biopsy, which had to be conducted in a separate building. Before I left the hospital premises, I gathered my courage to ask Dr Sam for his professional opinion. I knew that he and Dr Mike had several possible diagnoses running

Chapter 6: The Bump in the Road

through their minds. The tests they were ordering had to be in tandem with these.

"I know you don't have the facts yet and can't say conclusively what my condition is. But what are we testing for? Is lymphoma one of the hypotheses?" I asked bravely.

Dr Sam smiled kindly. "As you said, I can't say for sure until the results are out. The nasal biopsy will tell us if your nasopharyngeal area is the issue. The biopsy of the lump on your neck will help us identify the collection."

He hesitated before continuing. "Yes, lymphoma is a possibility. So is squamous cell carcinoma (SCC), commonly seen in Asians."

I swallowed hard. Either way, it was cancer.

I gave him a small smile and stuck my hand out. He accepted the gesture, and we shook hands.

"Thank you," I said gratefully. "I just needed to know what we're looking for, and if cancer was on the list of things. I appreciate your honesty and understand that nothing is conclusive until the results are out."

We waved Dr Sam and Dr Mike goodbye before proceeding to the other building where the neck biopsy — a fine needle aspiration (FNA) — was to take place. This procedure involved attaching a thin needle to a syringe and inserting it into the area of interest. Fluid/cells from the area were aspirated using the vacuum in the syringe and collected for further investigation.

The procedure hurt immensely. The pain was not unbearable, but the sensation felt like receiving an injection that was deliberately administered to cause as much pain as possible. The needle was withdrawn and reinserted several times in a quick fashion without being completely removed. At the best of times, needles and I are not good friends, so staying still throughout the procedure was a challenge. The only thing that kept me motionless on the hard, narrow bed was the sneaky suspicion that it would hurt more if I moved. What added to the discomfort was that the aspiration area had to be held down with firm, solid pressure once the needle was removed to prevent severe bruising, a task that a nurse who was present throughout carried out with grave responsibility.

To my unpleasant surprise, the procedure had to be performed on both sides of my neck.

"But I only have a lump on the right," I protested. I was feeling very much like a pincushion. This doctor had already pricked me in several different areas on the right side of my neck.

"We collect samples from both normal and abnormal areas on the same patient so that we can compare the tested area with your normal. We have to use your normal cells as a control, or it would be like comparing apples and oranges," he replied sympathetically.

Sigh. I knew this, but it didn't mean that I had to like it.

Resigned, I turned my head in the opposite direction.

After more than ten aspirations, he was finally finished.

"We won't be able to analyse your samples today as it's the end of the working week. I'm away next week, but my colleague will work on them. We deliver results directly to the ENT department, so you should hear from your doctor sometime next week." He stripped the gloves from his hands and tossed them into the bin.

Rod and I thanked him and the nurse for their time, wished them both a good weekend and left the building.

We walked to our parked car and drove away, heading towards Rod's workplace to drop him off. I pulled into a parking lot in front of the building so he could hop out.

"Are you okay?" He turned towards me. The drive to his workplace had been quiet, both of us lost in our own thoughts.

I nodded. I had numerous thoughts but needed time to process them all.

"Let's not worry about it until the results are out," he continued. He reached out to give me a tight hug.

"I know. I'm fine." I assured him with a small smile. "I'd better get going or I'll be late to pick the kids up from daycare. See you at home tonight."

He slid out of the car, and I drove off, waving at him in the rear mirror.

Ten minutes into the drive home, the tears started.

Although I had yet to receive the test results, the procedures I had undergone that day were confirmation. Although I knew it two days ago, I was now completely sure that it was lymphoma. It was just a matter of waiting for medical and scientific proof.

I didn't cry because it was lymphoma. Nor did I cry because I was afraid of dying.

I cried because I felt incredibly sorry and guilty.

I cried because I'd been such an idiot, and I had just realised it.

God had been talking to me after all. In fact, He wasn't just talking to me, He was showing me. He was, after all, a God of action. All the signs and symptoms I had experienced were His way of showing me that something was wrong. He had been trying to get my attention for ***months***, urging me back to the doctor again and again.

For the first time in months, I heard His voice clearly. It was as if a dam had broken, and His voice was finally audible. My mind was filled with visions of Him patiently speaking to me and waving in my face whilst I walked by, ignoring Him.

Amy, go back to the doctor. Get yourself another test. Amy, go back again. Don't give up. Insist on a diagnosis!

Every time I resigned myself to living with eczema, things got worse and I would go back to Dr Adam. Yet, instead of thanking Him for all the signs, I'd blamed Him for my physical distress. I'd screamed at God and complained about Him ignoring my plight. In my mind, it was His fault that He didn't interfere and His fault that I was living in misery. I had labelled Him uncaring, unmerciful and unfeeling when it was the exact opposite.

I was despicable, ungrateful, undeserving and yet, He didn't give up on me. What I had mistaken for silence was, in fact, evidence of His love and care.

Hindsight really is a wonderful thing. Knowing that God cares in theory is fact. Knowing that God cares on a deep, personal level and witnessing it being manifested in life is a revelation. I have, am, and always will be God's child. His love for me has never failed and will never fail. If I am not able to see or understand that truth, that is because of my own limitations and not His.

Knowing that God cares in theory is fact. Knowing that God cares on a deep, personal level and witnessing it being manifested in life is a revelation.

There was little I could do at that realisation but weep. I wept tears of repentance, of sorrow and of joy. My vision blurred, my nose watered, but mostly, my heart ached. I had to pull over twice. My tears blinded me, and I couldn't see the road clearly to drive. Both times, I leaned my forehead on the steering wheel and let my tears fall freely.

"I'm sorry. I'm so sorry. Please forgive me," I whispered over and over again.

I wished I had more time to sit with Him, to bask in His love and forgiveness, but I had a schedule to keep. I arrived home in the nick of time to pick the children up from daycare. By the time I reached my destination, my eyes were dry, and my soul was at peace. Just as I knew I had lymphoma, I also knew, deep down, that my God had forgiven me.

All was well between God and me.

CHAPTER 7

TALK ABOUT PERFECT TIMING

Every time I reflect on this time in my life, I cannot help but marvel at the way everything fell into place. Perhaps you may think me lucky and say that these were fortunate coincidences. However, for my family and I, it was divine provision. God really has the best timing. There was no amount of planning or orchestrating that could have pulled off what He did for me in this season.

In the week following the two biopsies, my cellphone never left my side. I needed to hear the confirmation of the lymphoma diagnosis from my doctor. Time dragged on slowly. I didn't receive a call on Monday.

Nothing on Tuesday either.

By Wednesday morning, I was biting my nails.

I wasn't just antsy about the test results. I was also concerned about our Christchurch and Wanaka holiday plans. Rod's month-long annual leave had been approved and we'd arranged to leave on Saturday that very week. Our travel plans and accommodation had been booked and paid for. If I wanted to cancel our plans, I had to do it soon or none of our payments would be refundable, partial or otherwise.

I called the ENT department on Wednesday and got through to the friendly receptionist. She didn't have any news for me but promised to tell Dr Sam that I'd called.

Despite the call, I didn't hear back from them that day. To be fair, I knew that they were extremely busy and that the call would have taken time out of the day that they didn't have.

Time was ticking, and the window for me to cancel our holiday plans was closing fast. The uncertainty was unsettling. I didn't want to cancel our plans if I wasn't required to be in Dunedin for tests or treatment. At the same time, I didn't want to postpone any tests or treatment plans for the sake of a little holiday. After discussing things, Rod and I resolved to put off cancelling our plans until we received definite word from the doctor. After all, it was just money that we risked losing.

I need not have worried because God had it all in hand.

On Thursday, I photographed what was to be my final portrait client for a long time — the job that, in essence, covered the cost of my ultrasound.

It was around 10 am on Friday, the 28th of February 2020, exactly one week from the day of the double biopsies, that I received my diagnosis. My phone rang while I was driving home after my shift at the local pool. I glanced at the screen: it was a call from a private, unlisted number.

Chapter 7 : Talk About Perfect Timing

It had to be the hospital.

I put my signal on, pulled toward the curb and parked the car. Turning off the engine, I answered the call.

Sure enough, it was Dr Sam with a confirmed diagnosis.

"It's Hodgkin's lymphoma."

Praise The Lord!

I don't think I know of anyone as pleased as I was to receive a cancer diagnosis.

I don't think I know of anyone as pleased as I was to receive a cancer diagnosis.

Those were the two words that I'd secretly hoped to hear since we left the appointment a week prior. My science background had provided me with sufficient information to know that there were two types of lymphoma: Hodgkin's and non-Hodgkin's. However, over the past week, further investigation on my part had revealed information that I was previously unaware of, that is, that Hodgkin's lymphoma is one of the most treatable cancers around. More than 90 per cent of Hodgkin's lymphoma patients survive for over five years after treatment. Typically, those with Hodgkin's lymphoma have a better outlook than those with non-Hodgkin's lymphoma.

For the past week, I'd secretly hoped that my diagnosis would be Hodgkin's lymphoma. I knew that God had my back and that He would work all things for good even if the cancer turned out to be malignant, but the sense of relief that accompanied the diagnosis with a better prognosis was overwhelming. It was as if a massive weight had been lifted off my shoulders.

"Thank you for letting me know. I'm so glad to finally get an answer."

"There are worse things one can have. This is one of the better cancers," he said sympathetically.

I had a small suspicion he said that to make me feel better. I liked Dr Sam; from what I observed the week before, he genuinely cared about his patients.

"I know," I responded with a small laugh. "I've googled it quite a bit. I was pretty sure it's lymphoma. I'm really thankful it's of the Hodgkin's variety!"

I think Dr Sam was a bit surprised at my enthusiasm upon receiving a cancer diagnosis. There was a startled silence before he asked me if I had any questions.

I did. In fact, I had plenty. "What do I do from here? What happens now?" I asked.

"Your diagnosis is not our department's speciality, so I've referred you to the haematology department. They will be in touch with you directly. I've also ordered several blood tests, which should be on your electronic health file by now. Call in to your medical practice sometime today to get those done so that we can forward the results to the department as soon as possible."

Chapter 7 : Talk About Perfect Timing

"I'll head there this morning," I replied, mentally creating a to-do list.

"I've also referred you for a PET/CT scan.[19] We don't have a PET facility in Dunedin, so you'll need to travel to Christchurch for this. The PET imaging department will give you a ring within the next day or two, but you should be in for a scan next week," he continued.

Next week in Christchurch?!?!

I barked out a startled half laugh-cry. If Dr Sam thought I'd gone mad, he displayed no audible indication. I couldn't hold my delight in — God had used our plans for His purposes again. His timing was indeed perfect. According to our holiday plans, we were going to be in Christchurch next week. I was thrilled beyond words, watching Him at work in our lives.

"That's absolutely perfect, thank you!" I exclaimed.

"No problem at all. Any other questions?"

"As a matter of fact, yes, just the one. Is there anything you can give me for the itch now that we have a definite diagnosis? To be honest, the lymphoma isn't bothering me that much at the moment. It's the itch that's killing me, figuratively speaking. It's really messing with my quality of life."

"Hmm, we can give you some antihistamines for that," he replied.

---

19 *A Positron Emission Tomography (PET)/Computed Tomography (CT) scan is a detailed, double scan (consisting of both the PET and CT) that is used to detect, diagnose and evaluate the progression of a disease on a molecular level. For more information, visit https://www.radiologyinfo.org/en/info/pet*

Been there, done that, I thought to myself.

"I'm already on antihistamines," I said out loud. "Is there nothing stronger you can give me?"

"There isn't much else that we can give you. The itch will disappear in time once the cause — the lymphoma — is treated. Unfortunately, it's a waiting game until then," he said apologetically.

"That's all good. Thank you so, so, much. I really appreciate your time and effort. Please also convey my thanks to Dr Mike."

"You're welcome. I will definitely do that. All the best with your treatment."

After our call, I sat in silence for a few minutes. A million different thoughts ran through my mind, but the main one that stood out was this: *I knew it*.

Deep in my gut, I was 99.99 per cent sure it was lymphoma before receiving the call. I'd known it, driving back from Dunedin, tears streaming down my face. Despite knowing then, a tiny part of me held on to the 0.01 per cent hope that it was a very stubborn case of eczema.

After all, eczema was better than cancer.

Hearing the confirmation, however, sealed the deal. It was now 100 per cent cancer.

I never thought that I'd have cancer. Then again, I don't think anyone is ever prepared to hear they have cancer. At the same time, I was relieved. So relieved to know that the persistent itching wasn't chronic eczema — I couldn't imagine having to live with this itch all my life. Or hay fever, which

Chapter 7 : Talk About Perfect Timing

would plague me year after year. As bad as cancer was, the prognosis for Hodgkin's was excellent and knowing that the itch would disappear in time gave me comfort.

I said a silent prayer of gratitude. I couldn't have asked for a better diagnosis, nor for it to happen at a better time. What were the odds of requiring a test in the exact city that we had planned to be in (which was, by the way, a six-hour drive away), and the exact same week?

I also prayed for strength to get through the day. I had a massive task ahead of me; breaking the news to my loved ones was going to be difficult. I decided to start with the easiest one: Rod. I called him on his work number.

"It's Hodgkin's!" I exclaimed triumphantly and tearfully.

He chuckled softly. "I guess Dr Sam called?"

"Yup. I just got off the phone with him."

"Hodgkin's is good news." Rod had been my lymphoma googling partner and understood the implications of a Hodgkin's diagnosis. "So, what next?"

I told him about the referral to haematology. Our conversation was subdued, but it wasn't heavy. We'd both had a week to come to terms with the possibility of cancer, so we were mentally and emotionally well prepared.

But there were two very important people in my life, with no prior notice of my condition, whom I now needed to share this news with.

"I should tell my parents now that we actually know what it is."

"Yes, definitely. Are you going to call once you get home?"

"I'll probably ring after lunch; it's still early in Malaysia." Being five hours behind New Zealand, it was barely six in the morning for my parents.

"Oh, that reminds me. Do we have to cancel our holiday plans?"

"That's the best part!" I excitedly told him about the PET/CT scan that was due to be scheduled in Christchurch.

"That's really good timing. We still get our holiday then," he said, pleasantly surprised.

"Right?! How blessed are we?"

"We are indeed. I have to get back to work, love. I'll see you when you get home and we'll talk," he said. "I love you."

"I love you too."

I hung up and sat in silence again. I was calm, but I wasn't ready to go home. I needed to talk to someone. I wanted a hug and someone to tell me that I was going to be okay. I knew the exact person to speak to.

I called a good friend and fellow lifeguard whom I had confided in throughout the whole itch-cough-lump journey. Joanna had witnessed my scratching and coughing for months and had known about my appointment the previous week. She had been my sounding board, this long-suffering friend of mine.

"What are you up to?" I asked her the moment she answered.

Chapter 7 : Talk About Perfect Timing

"I'm at The Warehouse, doing a collection for the Child Cancer Foundation," she replied.

"Oh."

I paused. There was no way to ease into it, so I dived right in.

"I just heard from the doctor. It's Hodgkin's," I blurted out.

"Are you OK? Do you want to come over for a chat?" she asked, concerned.

"I'm fine. I'm glad we know what it is for sure now and that we can work on a treatment rather than speculating," I replied. "How long are you at The Warehouse for?"

"Another 30 minutes or so."

"Cool, I'll come over for a bit."

I started up the car and headed for The Warehouse. When I got there, I spotted Joanna sitting behind a plastic table, a donation bucket and some stickers in front of her.

She waved me over. "Want to donate to the Child Cancer Foundation?"

"I do! But I don't have any cash on me." I laughed.

"Here, you can have a sticker regardless. For supporting the cause." She chuckled.

"Nah, save it for the people who actually donate," I said, taking a seat next to her. "Hey, what about adults with cancer? It's not all about the kids," I joked.

"Get your own fundraiser," she retorted.

I smiled, shrugged off my coat, and slung it on the back of the empty chair next to her. I sat down and we spoke about random topics — our children, work, the weather and life in general. After a few minutes of chatter, we fell silent.

Joanna looked at me carefully. "Would you like a hug?"

"Yes, please," I replied in a small voice.

We hugged for several long seconds. It felt really good. I was brimming with emotion, but I didn't feel like crying. I had released all my pent-up tears on the drive back from Dunedin the previous Friday. I was just relieved.

I told Joanna so after we separated.

"Of course you would feel that way. You finally know what it is, and it's not hay fever." She chortled sarcastically. "Hay fever! Couldn't be further from the truth. Now that you know what it is and that it can be treated, you can work on getting better."

"I've got so much to sort out, I'm not sure where to start. I'm not even sure what to do about work, the kids, my parents. I haven't told my parents yet…" I trailed into silence.

"Would you like me there as moral support when you call them?" Joanna looked at me searchingly.

I thought it over. "No, I think I'll be fine. It might be best to do it by myself, without Rod even. It's probably better for my parents, too. They'll feel more comfortable if they get emotional during our chat."

"If you're sure. Just ring if you need anything, OK?"

"I will. Thank you so much."

Chapter 7 : Talk About Perfect Timing

I looked at my watch. 11:30 am. "I'd better get going. I'm getting hungry, and I should get some food in me before I call the folks." I stood up and put my coat on.

After saying goodbye, I headed towards the health centre, completed all the blood work that Dr Sam had requested (the technician extracted quite a few vials of blood) and returned home.

1:25 pm

It was now 8:25 am in Malaysia. There was one person I wanted to notify before I called my parents. I placed the call and waited nervously while the phone rang.

My brother answered on the third ring. "Hi *che*.[20] What's up? You're calling early today."

"Hey. What are you up to?" I asked casually.

"Not much. Just getting ready to head to work."

"Do you have a few minutes to talk?"

"Sure," he said.

I took a deep breath and started talking. My brother remained attentive the entire time, only interrupting to ask a question here and there. I finished telling him my news and waited for a response. There was a long pause before he spoke.

"How are you feeling?" he asked.

---

20 *My brother's nickname for me. It is a short form for the term 'older sister' in Cantonese.*

"Rather relieved," I replied. "I've been unwell for such a long time that it's good to finally get a straight answer as to what it is!"

He chuckled. "And it can be treated?"

"Yes. I'm not sure what the full treatment regime is, I think it depends on the stage, but he did mention that it's one of the better ones to suffer from."

"That's good. I assume you'll tell Mum and Dad today?" he asked.

"That's the plan. I think I'll ring them later this morning, after they've had breakfast," I replied.

We spoke for another minute or so. He said to call if I needed any form of support and that he would pray for me. I told him I would, that I loved him, and hung up.

One down, one more to go.

4 pm

I had just dropped Lucas and Holly off at my in-laws', who live next door.

Distractions, gone.

It was now 11 am in Malaysia.

Time, suitable.

I could put it off no longer. I video called my mum on WhatsApp.

Chapter 7 : Talk About Perfect Timing

My mum answered after a few rings. "Amy! How are you?" she asked joyfully. "It's a funny time for you to call. Are the kids at daycare?"

"Hi Mum." I smiled. "No, they're at Rod's parents' place. How are you and Dad?"

We made small talk for a while. I told her about the kids' antics at home and in daycare, and my dad soon joined the conversation. After a few minutes, it was time to spill the beans.

"So…I have something to tell you. Can you please not interrupt me until I finish? I'm happy to answer any questions that you have after that."

"Of course," my dad said. My mum nodded in agreement. Their faces held identical expressions of curiosity and expectance.

For the second time that day, I recounted the tale. How the itch never went away, the reasons for not informing them, the many doctor appointments, the eczema diagnosis, the ultrasound, biopsies and fine needle aspirations, and finally, the phone call I received earlier that morning. My voice cracked a few times while relating the whole experience, but I managed to hold back tears. Both my parents listened in silence, their faces stoic and unrevealing. I couldn't tell what they were thinking, but I had a pretty rough idea. I held my breath after I finished.

My dad was the first to speak. "We have a lot of questions for sure, but the most important one is — are you okay?"

I smiled serenely. "I'm surprisingly all right. I'm not thinking 'Why me?' thoughts or that life is unfair. Cancer is totally random. It can affect anyone at any time, and I just so happen to be the one this time. If anything, I'm really blessed that it's Hodgkin's."

"That's a relief. It's a good attitude to have. Next question, when would you like us to come to you? We can take the next flight out."

I thought about it for a few long seconds. Finally, I said, "Maybe not yet. Not because I don't want you here, but I have no idea what's happening for the moment. I don't know what type of treatment is required, or when the treatment will start, or if I need to be an inpatient throughout the whole process or…" I trailed off and shrugged. "It might be better to wait until we know what the plan is before you make any travel arrangements. There's no point in you sitting around here if I'm not going to be at home for the next three months."

My parents saw the rationale behind that and agreed. We spoke for about another 20 minutes. Both my mum and dad had a lot of questions, but they were mostly questions that I didn't have answers to. I told them everything the doctor had told me and everything else I knew about Hodgkin's that I'd discovered online. I was quick to caution them against over-googling, as individual patient's circumstances, treatment, as well as responses to treatment are different. I told them to research it as I had done, but to only read the facts, not the speculations.

It felt good finally coming clean with my parents. It had been difficult to keep my itch from them and connect less with

Chapter 7 : Talk About Perfect Timing

them to avoid lying. This conversation was one more burden off my shoulders. Finally, I had to end the conversation; it was time to prepare dinner. Cancer or not, the children had to eat. Plus, I had some packing to do; we were going on a holiday tomorrow!

"You take good care of yourself, and keep us in the loop," my mum said.

"I definitely will. I'll also let you know as soon as we have a plan in place, and we can organise your trip here. I love you both."

"We love you too."

That evening, Rod and I went over to his parents and broke the news to them. Both my in-laws had beaten cancer in the past, so they had nothing but pure encouragement for me.

"I have no direct family history of cancer, so this must have come from your side," I joked. "How's that for truly being a part of the family?"

That remark earned me a few laughs and also several bone-crushing hugs.

I had God, and I had my family. I was going to get through this ordeal just fine.

I had God, and I had my family. I was going to get through this ordeal just fine.

Later that night, just before heading to bed, Rod and I read news of the first case of Covid-19 in New Zealand. I thought nothing of it at the time — thinking of it as another viral epidemic that would blow over before long — but the presence of Covid-19 was going to have a massive impact on our lives over the next few years.

Particularly over the course of my treatment.

CHAPTER 8

THE CANCER-MOON

Christchurch, what an amazing city! Prior to this trip, the only bit of Christchurch I'd seen and experienced was the airport. The many news reports of Christchurch as the earthquake-affected city had left me with a mental image of a city in ruins with not much to offer. Boy, was I surprised! Although there were signs and remains of earthquake damage, the city was thriving and definitely on the mend. The suburbs that were red-zoned — areas that were irreparably damaged and deemed unfeasible to rebuild on — looked like designated walking tracks with the return of Mother Nature and regrowth.

We rented a three-bedroom home for the length of our stay. The house was located in a residential area approximately ten minutes from the city centre. We had the whole property to ourselves, and most importantly, the rental included Netflix services. If you don't fully comprehend the importance of that statement, I'm going to hazard a guess that you don't have toddlers in your home. As much as I love my children and am against excessive screen time, Netflix is a very useful tool that Rod and I utilise when we are in dire need of children-free time.

We had arranged to stay in Christchurch for four nights, subject to any changes the PET/CT scan brought about. Rod and I were determined not to let my diagnosis ruin our family holiday. We visited tourist attractions, had picnics, went to the local markets, toured the city, ate until our stomachs felt like bursting and had a grand old time. The nagging itch, while still a thorn in my flesh, was made more bearable by our constant activity. Although the nights were still long, the fresh air and travels during the day combined with the effects of doxepin helped me fall asleep a little easier.

We were at a wildlife reserve on Monday when I received a call from the radiology department in Christchurch. The kids were having a ball feeding the various birds and animals that were free to roam the grounds. Lucas was, in fact, a touch violent with his generosity. He threw the birdfeed at the birds with gusto; it must have seemed like a hailstorm to the little ones. I walked over to a quiet corner to converse with the receptionist.

After introducing herself and asking me several personal questions to confirm my identity, she dived right into the heart of things. "Dr Sam mentioned that you're in Christchurch this week…?" she trailed off inquiringly.

"Yes, we are. We're already here, so anytime from today would be great," I replied.

Chapter 8 : The Cancer-moon

Dr Sam had told me it would most likely be this week, but nothing was confirmed until the radiology department officially verified my appointment.

"We have you scheduled for 9:30 am on Wednesday. Does that suit?"

She couldn't see me, but I felt a massive grin stretch across my face. This had to be God's provision, as the timing couldn't have been more perfect. Rod and I had originally planned to leave for Wanaka after lunch on Wednesday. When I had heard about the scan from Dr Sam, I was aware that we may have to extend our stay in Christchurch, depending on the time and day it was scheduled for. With it now officially scheduled for the morning, our plans were intact.

"That's perfect, thank you!" I exclaimed.

"There are a few things you need to know about the procedure, is this a good time to talk?" she asked me.

I turned to look at the kids, who were blissfully unaware that I had stepped away. Both Lucas and Holly were still preoccupied with the feeding frenzy. I signalled to Rod that this was going to take a while and returned my attention to the call.

"Yes, now is great."

She spent a few minutes explaining the PET/CT scan to me: what it was, what to expect and why it was required for my situation. Then she gave me some instructions to follow in preparation for the appointment.

"You'll need to fast for six hours prior to the scan, and drink at least a litre of water in the two hours prior to the appointment. Don't exercise or take any long walks beforehand. Wear loose and comfortable clothing, preferably without any metal bits in it. If you prefer, we'll have a hospital gown that you can change into."

I took mental notes and uttered the occasional agreement to signal that I was still listening. "On the day, we'll get you to fill in some forms and sign a consent form for the procedure. We'll hook you up with an intravenous line and inject you with the radioactive substance. Then you'll be asked to lie quietly on a comfortable reclining armchair for about 60 to 90 minutes, so feel free to get some shut eye then."

"I get to have a nap before my scan?" I asked in disbelief.

"Yes, it would be ideal if you can nap. We want your muscles nice and relaxed so that they don't show up as a false positive during imaging."

"You won't have to ask me twice!" I said, laughing. "I have two very energetic toddlers, so naps are currently non-existent for me."

"Oh, that's great! Some rest time for you," she replied with a smile in her voice. "You mentioned your children, so it's important to note that you'll be radioactive for approximately four hours after the injection. During this time, you should avoid being in close proximity to children and pregnant women. The scan will take about two hours from your injection to complete, so upon leaving the premises, you'll need to stay away from your children for another two hours or so."

This whole procedure was starting to sound better and better. First a nap, and then some enforced 'me' time? It sounded like a spa day. Bring on Wednesday!

Chapter 8 : The Cancer-moon

"There is no cost attached to the scan. There will, however, be a cost if you fail to attend or cancel your scan within 24 hours of your scheduled date, which cannot be billed to insurance. This is to recoup the cost of the radioactive substance, which is produced in Wellington and has to be flown in specifically for you on the day," she continued. "Should the radioactive material not make it down on the day due to a flight cancellation or disruptive weather conditions, we will ring you as soon as possible to reschedule your appointment."

That made sense.

"You'll also be able to recoup a portion of your travel expenses for making the trip to Christchurch for your scan. Your doctor will be able to give you more information and provide you with the paperwork, so just ask them for the forms when you get back home."

Whoa. That was totally unexpected. At the same time, it was a tremendous blessing. We had budgeted for this trip, but every little bit counted, especially with my upcoming treatment regime and timeframe still uncertain.

This was yet another gift from God. He really did have it all worked out for good.

We ended the conversation, and I said yet another silent prayer of thanks. These thanksgiving prayers were becoming a frequent occurrence as the events continued to unfold. Despite having cancer, I was overwhelmed with gratitude. Everything was falling perfectly into place. I was able to go in for the scan, spend a couple of hours by myself, and then leave Christchurch with my family according to our plans. The timing couldn't have been more perfect. I felt as if I was playing a game of Tetris, and although I had been given various tile pieces that I wasn't quite sure how to fit into the allocated space, I didn't have to worry because God was playing the game with me.

I felt as if I was playing a game of Tetris, and although I had been given various tile pieces that I wasn't quite sure how to fit into the allocated space, I didn't have to worry because God was playing the game with me.

I turned up at the radiology department at the scheduled time on Wednesday. After being ushered into the waiting room, I was given a lengthy form to fill out on an iPad. There were various questions on medical history — past surgeries, medication allergies, chemotherapy history, family history, and so on. I was then provided with a hospital gown to change into and led into a dimly lit room with the most comfortable reclining chair I'd ever sat on. It was large, plush, and as it was powered by electricity, it responded to the lightest touch. Adjusting the recline on the armchair gave new meaning to the phrase "not having to lift a finger" — I literally didn't have to lift mine!

Chapter 8 : The Cancer-moon

The technician gave me an intravenous line on my left arm, injected the radioactive substance and left me to my own devices for an hour. The lights were turned off, the blinds were shut, and there was soft music playing through the speakers. If it weren't for the fact that I was still itching, that hour of rest would have been utter bliss.

After the hour, I was requested to empty my bladder. I was then directed to the room that housed the machine. It was a large, white room with the scanner situated in the middle. I was instructed to lie with my arms raised above me on a horizontal platform, which was inserted into the hollow end of a cylindrical tube.

Although this was a foreign experience for me, I could tell it was just another routine day at the office for the technicians: their movements were fluid and precise as they positioned and hooked me up to the respective equipment. They also had music playing from the speakers to minimise the loud whirring of the machine. It's true that we form strong associations between songs/music and life events. Since that day, I've not been able to hear the song, 'Daydream Believer' by The Monkees without vividly recalling my first ever PET/CT scan.

The scan took approximately 30 minutes. After the scan, I changed back into my own clothing and was informed that the results would be sent to my doctor as soon as possible. I spent the next two hours sightseeing and strolling the streets of Christchurch. Later that afternoon, we drove away from Christchurch to Wanaka, where our holiday was meant to continue.

We didn't know it then, but our trip was about to be cut short.

Wanaka is a town located approximately an hour's drive northeast of Queenstown, which is renowned for being home to the adventure bucket list. Touted as a smaller version of Queenstown, local and international tourists who prefer a calmer and more peaceful atmosphere flock to this destination. Like Queenstown, Wanaka boasts a host of adventure sports or activities for visitors. It was the perfect place to end our mini holiday or our 'cancer-moon', as Rod called it.

We had barely taken a bite of our breakfast on Thursday morning — an award-winning pie from Kai Pai Bakery, whose chicken, leek and bacon pie won a Gold Award in the 2019 & 2021 NZ Supreme Pie Awards — when I received a call from an oncologist in Dunedin. My internal alarm bells started ringing again. This was the second time I'd been contacted within 24 hours of a test, a sign that things were serious. The speed at which I was being notified of test results was truly alarming.

Rod walked the kids over to the nearby playground to keep them occupied while I sought refuge in the stillness of our parked car, my award-winning pie forgotten.

"Your scan results are out."

I braced myself for the worst.

"There are tumours around the clavicle region where your neck lump was, extensive involvement of your right lung (note:

Chapter 8 : The Cancer-moon

I found out later that there was a massive tumour in the lung, which explained my chronic cough) and an accumulation of fluid around your heart. The latter is particularly worrying because it's constricting your heart and causing it to work harder than it needs to."

Uh oh.

I had been experiencing shortness of breath and an accelerated heart rate that accompanied all my light activities for a few weeks now but had attributed those to my declining fitness level. After all, I had not been exercising due to what I believed were eczema issues. I mentioned that and the occasional lightning sensations in my back to the oncologist.

"There isn't anything on the scan that is an obvious cause for the back sensations. However, I'm not ruling out Hodgkin's as the cause of those as well, in which case they will disappear once your treatment commences. As for the shortness of breath, that is most likely due to the fluid accumulation around the heart. You will need to take things easy for the next week. The fluid should start draining once your treatment begins, but we can arrange to have it drained if we need to. Make sure you don't do any vigorous exercise or exert yourself in any way," she advised.

"Okay. What do we do from here?"

"We're arranging a biopsy surgery for you now. We need a larger tissue sample to determine the exact lymphoma classification so we can start planning your treatment. It will have to be under general anaesthesia, so you'll be admitted as an inpatient for the surgery. Keep an eye on your phone for the call," she told me.

"We're in Wanaka at the moment," I responded hesitantly. "We're headed back to Balclutha on Saturday. Should we return home today just in case I'm called in?"

"No, you should be fine. We probably won't be able to get you on the surgery schedule until early next week. Just be careful, especially since you're away from home. Is there a hospital in Wanaka?" she asked me.

Good question.

"I have no idea," I admitted.

"Hmmm, I'm looking it up now, and it looks like there isn't one. The nearest hospital is in Queenstown. If you feel unwell, take yourself there immediately. Let them know your condition, and they can get in touch with us."

She cautioned me to take things easy, and we ended the conversation. I sat in the car quietly for a brief minute. That conversation had unnerved me. I didn't realise that my condition was that serious. The lung and especially the heart condition sounded grave. Something as simple as an increased heart rate meant so much more than just strenuous physical activity.

After sharing the news with my husband and finishing my now stone-cold breakfast, Rod and I took the kids to a large nearby playground. Throughout our trip and all our sightseeing, I was fortunate that we had been exploring at a snail's pace because there was plenty to do and see. The playground, however, was a different kettle of fish altogether. Lucas and Holly, with their short attention spans, ran from one set of equipment to another — the swings, the seesaw,

Chapter 8 : The Cancer-moon

the slides — they wanted to do them all at once. To keep them within our sights, Rod actively trailed them while I sauntered after him.

That was when I realised that I was panting.

Normally, I would have brushed it off. I was aware, after all, that my fitness level was at an all-time low. However, I was fresh from a conversation with the oncologist and decided to check on my heart rate using my watch just in case. I was thankful for wearable modern technology; what did we use to do before smartwatches?! Tapping on the love-heart icon on the screen, I waited while it recorded my heart rate. After several seconds, my watch vibrated, and I glanced at the number glowing on the screen.

It registered at over 100 beats per minute.

Whoa.

My normal resting heart rate registers in the low 70s. A heart rate of over 90 usually meant I was undergoing some form of moderate exercise. A hundred was rare for me, especially since I wasn't a massive fan of vigorous, intense exercise.

And all I had done was take a stroll in the park. Literally.

I showed Rod the reading on my watch, and he raised his eyebrow in surprise.

"Hmmm. That's a bit high, isn't it?" he asked.

"Quite. That's not normal for me," I replied.

We watched in silence for a while as the children bounced each other up and down on the seesaw.

"You should call your doctor and ask her if that's a concern. We should maybe head home today," he suggested.

"Today?" I echoed.

"We're not having much fun anyway, now that we know the severity of your condition. Plus, the uncertainty of not knowing the area well and being away from home is another concern. We had a good time in Christchurch. Let's just head home to familiar surroundings, stay put for the weekend, and rest up for the week to come."

"I'd hate to cut our holiday short, though. We've barely seen any of Wanaka," I protested weakly.

"We'll be back, love. Wanaka will always be here; it's only a three-hour drive away from us. We can come back anytime." Rod smiled gently.

I kept silent for a long minute. Rod was right. I yearned to be in the comfort of our own home. At the same time, I was reluctant to end our holiday as that marked the end of our escape from reality. Going home meant facing the music and dealing with cancer.

"I'll drop you off at our hotel room after lunch so you can get some rest and call the doctor. Then I'll take the kids to the pool, let them burn off some energy and we can head home after, just in time for the kids' dinner and bedtime. What do you say?"

I nodded. "Okay, let's go home."

I couldn't reach my doctor that afternoon but left a message with the receptionist on duty. I packed our bags while the kids were at the pool, and we headed home to Balclutha that afternoon.

Chapter 8 : The Cancer-moon

"It's good that you're home. We think it's in your best interests to be monitored over the weekend."

It was late Friday morning. I'd just answered a call from the doctor at the oncology unit in Dunedin hospital. They'd had a team meeting earlier that morning and collectively decided it was advisable for me to be admitted that very day. It was fortunate we got home the night before.

"Okay. What time should I be there?"

"Can you make it before noon? Report to unit 8C on level eight; they'll be expecting you."

"I'll be there. Thank you for calling."

Rod looked at me questioningly. He had been listening in on the conversation since I answered the phone.

"Are we going to the hospital?" he asked with raised eyebrows.

I nodded mutely.

"Just pack the essentials for tonight. We'll visit tomorrow and bring you everything else that you need. I'll bring the kids over to my folks and let them know we're off to the hospital." He looked at me carefully. "You okay?"

"Yeah, I'm fine. I just thought we would get more time together this weekend, so this is a little unexpected." I smiled up at him.

"I doubt there will be much happening over the weekend. We'll visit tomorrow, and maybe we can do something together in Dunedin for the day," he reassured me.

I quickly tossed a few things into an overnight bag while Rod ushered the children next door to his parents. We were both ready to go in record time. There was, however, one stop I needed to make before heading to the hospital: the local pool.

I had to break the news to my fellow lifeguards. Michelle, our manager, already knew — Joanna had delivered the news at my request while we were in Christchurch — but the rest of the team were still in the dark. Being a small team, we were close, and I owed them an explanation for what was going to be an extended absence. Especially since they were going to have to cover my shifts between themselves.

We pulled up into a parking bay at the facility, and I motioned for Rod to stay in the car. I walked into the building to see four of them gathered at the reception area. I stole a quick glance at the pool. It was relatively quiet, as it usually was just before lunch hour.

"What do you need to tell us? We've been going nuts trying to guess your news. Just tell us already, won't you?" Sarah asked before I could say a word.

I laughed out loud. I had told the team before leaving on our holiday that I had some serious news to share. I'd planned to tell them once our holiday ended but had not expected the speed at which I needed to be admitted.

All of them looked at me expectantly. I tried to speak, but hesitated.

Where should I start?

Joanna looked at me carefully. "Do you want me to tell them?" she asked me gently.

Chapter 8 : The Cancer-moon

"No, I can do it." I shook my head with a smile.

There was no easy way to say it, so I just blurted it out.

"I have cancer," I said bluntly. "The itch, the cough, the lump, the back pains, all the symptoms that some of you have been hearing about for some time: they're all cancer-related. Not hay fever. The doctor called me this morning, advising me to be admitted, so I'm on my way to the hospital now."

All of them knew that I had been experiencing a whole-body itch for a while (it was impossible not to scratch throughout a whole shift), but I don't think they expected to hear that. Both Sarah and Jane looked shocked. There was a stunned silence.

Sarah broke the silence first.

"I thought you were going to tell us that Rod is cheating on you! Or that you are leaving him! Or something crazy like that!" she exclaimed, half laughing and half crying.

I laughed, tears in my eyes. "No, he is most definitely not cheating on me. Is this news any less crazy?"

Sarah leaned forward and engulfed me in a bone-crushing hug. It was exactly what I needed, and for that I was grateful.

"It's just as crazy. Definitely not what we expected to hear." She released me and rubbed my arms. "How are you feeling?"

I grinned. "Surprisingly fine. I've had time to process this over the past week."

I told them about the diagnosis call, the scan on Wednesday, and the phone call I received earlier that morning. All of them listened attentively.

"So the itch and the cough are because of cancer?" Jane asked.

I nodded. "Yup. Who would have thought, right?"

I glanced at my watch. "I'd better run. We have an hour-long drive, and I told the doctor that I'd be in before noon."

I looked at Michelle. "Thank you so much for arranging cover for my shifts. I'll be in touch once I know the treatment regime. There are plenty of people who work throughout their cancer treatment; I hope I can be one of them."

Michelle nodded. "Just let me know when you find out. Don't worry about work, between us we have your shifts covered until you get back." She reached out and gave me a hug.

Michelle was the best boss ever, and I had the best work and support team in the world.

After one last hug from Joanna, I waved all of them goodbye and walked out the sliding doors into the sunshine.

It was time to head to the hospital.

PART 3

THE HOSPITAL

CHAPTER 9

8C, THE ONCOLOGY WARD OF DUNEDIN HOSPITAL

Cancer patient. A label that no one ever aspires to or welcomes. It definitely wasn't an identity I'd expected to acquire in my lifetime. However, it had been given to me, whether I liked it or not. My condition and circumstances were beyond my control, but I had a choice in my perspective and how I decided to live out the experience. I made it my goal to live my life in a way that would be a testimony to God's transforming power and love. I could only hope and pray fervently that I'd live up to the challenge.

My condition and circumstances were beyond my control, but I had a choice in my perspective and how I decided to live out the experience.

Despite my sobering circumstances, I was extremely grateful that I had the opportunity to step foot in the oncology ward. So many others have gone on before me that had incurable types and stages of cancer. I'd had the good fortune to be diagnosed with a curable variety. There was also a time in history when humans possessed insufficient medical knowledge or technology to treat what we now deem curable cancers. In fact, the first successful cures of advanced Hodgkin's lymphoma were only reported in 1964, a mere half a century ago.[21] The treatment regimen for Hodgkin's lymphoma has since been improved and fine-tuned, and I was truly blessed to be born in the decade that I was.

No, I don't think I want to disclose which decade that was. Never ask a lady her age.

Rod and I reported to the oncology ward just after lunch and were escorted through immediately; they had been expecting me. Once again, I was astounded at the speed at which events were occurring. It was yet another reminder that my condition was to be taken seriously. I was officially admitted into the ward and subjected to a flurry of tests. The first was a blood test. I was told somewhat apologetically that blood tests were going to be routine from now on. Needles were going to be a constant companion throughout this journey. True to their word, there seemed to be double the amount of collection vials compared to the average blood test.

---

21 *https://www.hematology.org/about/history/50-years/cure-of-hodgkin-lymphoma*

Chapter 9: 8C, The Oncology Ward of Dunedin Hospital

Following the blood tests, I was given an urgent echocardiogram. The PET/CT scan images had revealed the presence of pericardial effusion (a scientific term for the buildup of fluid around the heart), and the echocardiogram was necessary to determine if the fluid had to be drained before the weekend in order to ease the pressure on my heart. I personally found it fascinating that the pericardial space was so extensively involved and mentioned that to the technician. He reminded me that lymphoma was a form of blood cancer and involved the lymphatic system, a part of the body's circulatory system, which could affect any organ.

Hmm true.

Imagine if I'd lost my life due to a heart complication even before treatment began.

He also informed me that if the echocardiogram revealed an acceptable level of fluid, the doctors might decide to allow the fluid to drain naturally with treatment of the lymphoma. It was a matter of balancing risk factors and selecting the best course of action. It was best to avoid any invasive procedure — no matter how little — that wasn't completely necessary.

That made sense.

After the echocardiogram, I was assigned a bed in a private room, yet another of the 'this is serious' red flags. I still recall sharing a room in the maternity unit with another new mother after delivering Lucas. I remember being surprised and a teeny, tiny, wee bit anxious (Okay, I admit that I was very anxious) about having to share a room. Not because of the sharing, but because I was a first-time mum, and I had no clue as to why my baby was crying continually.[22]

Having to share a hospital room with another (also first-time) mum made things difficult for us both because the moment one baby started crying, the other would wake up to join in. I doubt either of us (or our babies) got much sleep the two nights we were in hospital. Based on that experience, I knew that private hospital rooms were a precious commodity and not given out lightly. So as much as I was pleased about not having to share a room, the privilege of privacy also filled me with dread.

They probably don't make cancer patients share because one sick (read: throwing up) patient would trigger the rest to follow suit, and that wouldn't do. I shuddered at the thought.

It wasn't long before the echocardiogram results were out. Rod and I were informed that the draining was unnecessary at this stage but that I was to be monitored over the weekend and all strenuous activity to be avoided. I was, again, told to report any form of pressure in the chest region or breathing difficulties to the doctor on duty.

Rod and I were then left to our own devices for about an hour before two young doctors entered and informed me that they were going to wheel me down for a tissue biopsy that very same day.

---

22 *Lucas terrified me during his first few days on earth. In fact, he still terrifies me daily with some of the things he does. I have been told, on various occasions, that this will be a lifetime malady.*

Chapter 9: 8C, The Oncology Ward of Dunedin Hospital

"Today? I thought it was going to be next week because it needs to be done under general anaesthesia?" I was surprised. This turn of events was completely unexpected.

"We changed plans because of your echocardiogram results," one of the doctors said. "Due to the pericardial effusion, we're afraid your heart may be at risk if we put you under general anaesthesia."

Wow. I hadn't considered that. Imagine if I never woke up from that procedure.

"Dr Tim here managed to sweet-talk the biopsy team into conducting a punch biopsy for you before they clock out for the weekend. You're going to be their last procedure this evening," he continued.

I laughed. "Thank you so much! If not for you, I'd have had to wait until next week, wouldn't I?"

Dr Tim looked proud but embarrassed.

I had one last question for them. "Will this procedure be as accurate as the general one?"

The doctor who had spoken looked thoughtful. "It's hard to say. The amount of tissue we'll be able to remove may be significantly less, so it depends on how lucky we are with the quality of the sample."

In a matter of what seemed like minutes after the doctors left my room, I was wheeled down several floors to an intimidating room with a screen, lots of imaging equipment and friendly medical professionals. The doctor in charge filled me in on the procedure and the details. It basically involved some local anaesthetic injected with what looked like a massive needle, an incision around the site of the swelling and a tissue punch taken from the area of interest. The doctor assured me that the local anaesthetic would keep me completely numb.

"You will, however, hear a really loud noise. I'll let you know before you hear it, so that you won't be taken aback and jerk in surprise." She demonstrated the biopsy instrument with a loud clack.

I nodded my understanding. It wouldn't pay to make any sudden movements during a procedure involving a sharp instrument and an area close to my respiratory tract.

She handed me a form on a clipboard. I took it and started scanning through the contents.

"We will need you to sign a consent form, saying that we've given you the relevant information and that you agree to the procedure. You will have a tiny scar from the incision, but it should just be a small one approximately this long." She pointed the tip of her thumb to the first groove on her pinkie. "Do you have any questions?"

I looked up at her with a sudden grin. "Just one important one. Can I eat as usual after the procedure?"

The doctor smiled. Rod laughed and said, "You've got your priorities straight!"

"It's a valid question!" I chuckled defensively.

I was assured that the procedure would not affect my diet. I'd been fairly sure that it wouldn't. Even if it did, I wasn't too concerned about food. It was a nervous joke.

Chapter 9: 8C, The Oncology Ward of Dunedin Hospital

Yes, I was nervous.

I signed the papers and the biopsy commenced. The local anaesthetic worked a treat; I couldn't feel a thing. I have to admit, the loud punches were a bit jarring. It was one thing to hear the noise while the doctor held the punch instrument a person's width away, but another when it was right next to my right ear. The doctors were amazing, though, and warned me prior to each punch so that I was prepared. Rod held my hand throughout the procedure. Grateful, I gripped his hand tightly as my source of courage and strength.

I don't remember how many tissue punches they took, but it was enough for me to lose count. Soon enough, we were done. I thanked the doctors for staying past their working hours on a Friday evening. All of them were very gracious and said that it wasn't a problem. The orderly was called, and I was wheeled back up to my room with a brand-new bandage on my right clavicle.

Thanks to Dr Tim arranging my tissue biopsy before the weekend, I was now allowed medication. Finally! The doctors had been reluctant to prescribe me any before the procedure because they didn't want to shrink the tumour prior to sampling. However, now that the laboratory had all the samples they needed in order to classify and grade my disease, they could begin treating me. Oral chemotherapy medication, while in itself is incomplete as a form of therapy, is sufficient to begin tumour lysis (a medical term for death of cancer cells). I was really excited to be on medication because apart from the obvious reason — kicking cancer's butt — I was hopeful that the initial oral treatment would alleviate the chronic symptoms that had been bothering me: the itch, cough and the lightning sensations across my back.

I greeted the nurse who walked in armed with medication with obvious delight. I had been seeking relief for months, and I was finally going to have some!

She placed a little paper cup on my bedside table alongside a little white plastic tub of cream and tapped on the tub. "This one here is a moisturiser laced with menthol, a chemical that produces a fresh and cooling sensation on the skin. It is only for transient relief, though. Use it as needed until the effects of your medication kick in. Once the drugs start producing results, your itch symptoms should naturally disappear."

Pointing at the little paper cup, she continued, "I also have a few pills for you here." I peered over the rim of the cup.

A few?!?!

I couldn't count them from my vantage point, but there were at least two layers of pills of various colours, shapes and sizes stacked together in that little vessel. The bottom of the cup was covered by pills. The nurse was either really used to dispensing a large number of pills at a time or just really good at downplaying the number of pills for my benefit. In this ward, I suspected that the former was true.

Chapter 9: 8C, The Oncology Ward of Dunedin Hospital

After a short explanation of the various pills and the role they would play in my treatment,[23] the nurse left me. I studied the contents of the paper cup more closely and let out a little teary laugh. Here was yet another piece of evidence that God had been present this whole time. Sitting in the little paper cup, nestled amongst larger white pills, were four tiny circular pink pills.

It was prednisone.

The nurse had explained that prednisone is one of the crucial drugs used to combat and treat Hodgkin's lymphoma. This drug was the exact steroid that Dr Adam had prescribed weeks ago in an attempt to calm the effects of what we thought was eczema at the time. It was no wonder the pills had worked so well then; we were unknowingly treating the cancer!

Had Dr John given in to my request for more oral steroids, my physical symptoms would not have progressed the way they did. The lump on my clavicle may not have appeared, and the cancer would have progressed undetected. It could have been disastrous! I shuddered at the thought and said yet another silent prayer of thanks to God.

Over the course of the weekend, I became very adept at swallowing whole handfuls of pills. It became a little game of sorts for me, to see if I could swallow the entire contents of

---

23 *Several of the pills that I recall being prescribed: prednisone (an oral steroid), allopurinol (to prevent the effects of tumour lysis syndrome and high levels of uric acid), valaciclovir (an antiviral), Trisul (an antibiotic), promethazine (an antihistamine), loratadine (another antihistamine), and codeine (a cough suppressant).*

every cup the nurse brought me in one go. Some cups were more challenging than others, but I always managed. It's a pity that it wasn't a skill that I was particularly proud of.

Another addition to my daily routine was a suggested minimum daily liquid intake. I was ordered (albeit very kindly) to keep myself hydrated and prescribed a continual IV drip to prevent tumour lysis syndrome (TLS). TLS is a potentially life-threatening condition that occurs due to the inability of the kidneys to process excessive levels of cancer metabolites in the bloodstream at the same speed at which they are released. Tumour lysis occurs when large numbers of cancer cells die within a short period of time due to medication. This large massacre causes the contents of these abnormal cells to leach into the bloodstream, producing a surge in levels of undesired substances. The drip and my increased fluid intake were essential to helping my kidneys flush these metabolites from my system.

I became very proficient at conducting my day-to-day activities while being hooked up to a saline drip. Everywhere I went, the drip went with me. If you've seen hospital TV shows where the patients walk around hooked up to IV lines and IV poles on wheels, you can rest in the knowledge that those scenes are 100 per cent legit. The only time I was allowed reprieve from my constant companion was in the shower.

True to the nurse's word on the first day at the hospital, needles and I became very well acquainted. My blood was drawn at least once daily, and there were occasions where a new IV line had to be inserted because the existing one developed a clot at the puncture site. I was told that my blood

Chapter 9: 8C, The Oncology Ward of Dunedin Hospital

clotting factors were excellent as I seemed to require a new line each time I had a shower, no matter how quick I was.

Apart from the pills, IV lines and needles, the rest of the weekend passed quietly. The little pink magic prednisone pills worked wonders. Because the oral cancer-fighting-tumour-shrinking dose was higher than the eczema-treatment dose that Dr Adam had prescribed, the itch nightmare and skin rash that had plagued me for months melted away almost overnight as if it had never happened. It was really quite anti-climactic.

Rod, Lucas and Holly came to visit on Saturday. I was informed that I was allowed to leave for short periods of time as long as I stayed hydrated and close to the hospital. Each departure from hospital grounds meant a new IV line upon my return, though, so I had to be selective with my excursions. Was my love for the kids sufficient to warrant yet another needle? It was! I happily left the hospital to spend the day with them in town.

It was during lunch — when the kids were seated long enough for us to hold onto their attention — that Rod and I told them both that Mummy was going to be in hospital for a few days and that Daddy was going to be in charge at home. We explained that I was a little ill and needed the doctor's care for a few days longer than usual but that I would be home really soon. They both nodded their little heads and were excited that Daddy wasn't going to work for a while, especially since Mummy wouldn't be around to spoil their fun. After all, Daddy is the fun parent in our home. It wasn't long before they lost interest in the subject altogether.

Just before they left for the day, Holly gave me a cuddle and a very adult-like pat on the hand with grave instructions to take care of myself and to feel better soon. Lucas told me to "Listen to the doctors and take your medicine, Mummy."

I am very blessed to have two amazing children. I often reflect on this time and consider myself fortunate to have been diagnosed when they were so young. They have close to no recollection of the period where Mummy wasn't home for an extended period, nor did they worry excessively because they didn't truly comprehend the gravity of a cancer diagnosis. We didn't even mention the word cancer because Lucas was at the age of questioning everything, and cancer would have been a difficult concept to explain (unless we were up to fielding the many 'But why?' questions that were bound to follow).

I often reflect on this time and consider myself fortunate to have been diagnosed when they were so young.

After Rod and the kids had left, I was once again struck by God's ability to work our human plans out for good. Thanks to the month-long leave that Rod had applied for prior to my diagnosis, we didn't have to scramble to make alternative childcare arrangements for the next few weeks. Everything was in complete alignment. We couldn't have planned it better ourselves.

Chapter 9: 8C, The Oncology Ward of Dunedin Hospital

I spent what I thought was my last pretreatment weekend catching up on sleep and resting. I was at peace: I had a diagnosis, treatment was going to commence soon and, most importantly, I only had myself to care for in the hospital. There were no needy children around, I had no chores to do, and I even had 'room service' deliver meals to me three times a day! Truth be told, apart from the fact that I was ill and had to lug an IV pole with me everywhere I went, it was quite a restful period. I was finally getting some quality rest now that the itch was subsiding. I could even watch all the Korean drama I wanted to, instead of the normal Paw Patrol I was subjected to at home. It was bliss!

God must have known that I needed some rest and relaxation because as it happened, the next week ended up being a whirlwind of activity.

Monday morning in the hospital started with a group of doctors filing into my room. Rod had come to visit (sans children) and managed to get there just in time for the briefing. The doctor in charge of my case (Dr Fiona) introduced herself and the rest of the team before filling me in on the discussion that had taken place about me that very morning during their meeting.

"Your biopsy results are not out yet. We're hoping to get the results before commencing treatment to ensure you're on the right regime. In the meantime, there are several tests that we need to conduct prior to your treatment starting. We're ordering you a lung function test as you have a large tumour in your right lung and a dental check to ensure your teeth and gums are in good condition. We need to make sure you are not prone to potential infection as you will be immunocompromised once chemotherapy begins."

I had to give it to the doctors, they were really thorough. As a cancer patient, a dental examination was the last thing I expected.

"You'll also need a PICC[24] line inserted; it's an IV line that goes through your arm to the central blood system. Your PICC line will be the route through which the chemotherapy is administered, and we will be able to draw blood from you via the same catheter, which means fewer needles for you. We've arranged for this to be done as soon as possible. For now, we'll continue with the tumour lysis procedure. You'll need to keep your fluid intake up and hang tight until the biopsy results are out. The nurses will come by later with some written material for you to read and some information on the various types of support that are available."

Dr Fiona looked at me kindly. "Do you have any questions?"

I had a million questions. This whole experience was new to me, but I knew that I was likely just a routine case for an oncology doctor. I looked at the team supporting me in my recovery, and I knew I was in safe hands.

"I have plenty of questions, but you've covered the important parts. I'm guessing some of my questions will be answered in the written information that the nurses will bring me?"

---

24 *PICC stands for Peripherally-Inserted Central Catheter and is pronounced as 'pic'.*

Chapter 9: 8C, The Oncology Ward of Dunedin Hospital

Dr Fiona smiled. "Yes, they will. If you have questions at any time, don't hesitate to ask any of the nurses here. You will also see one of us every morning when we do our ward rounds, so if you think of anything, we're here to help."

Rod and I thanked them, and the whole group filed out of the room as quickly as they had arrived.

Rod turned to look at me. "More waiting then. At least things are moving now, and you'll be able to get a bit more rest before chemotherapy starts."

I nodded. "I slept really well over the weekend now that my itch is starting to subside. A few more days of respite will be good before treatment."

I peered at my husband's face. He looked a little weary, and my heart went out to him. I could tell that this whole experience was taking a toll on him. He had to care for me and our children in my absence, so the least I could do was keep my own company while in hospital to save him the daily two-hour drive.

"I'll be fine by myself. I have everything I need here, and if I do need anything I will let you know. Why don't you stay home and spend some time with the kids? Feel free to come in with them to visit, but don't feel like you have to be here every day."

"I'll bring the kids in for a visit soon," he said, rubbing his neck. "You're right, it is a lot of driving. I'll pop by again in a couple of days. If you need me for anything at all, just call and I'll be here."

FINDING ME | 153

I reassured him that I would be just fine. He stayed for a few more hours and gave me a tight hug before he left. Once by myself, I turned the TV on to find something interesting to watch, only to find the news on. The main coverage was the Covid-19 virus and its rapid spread throughout the world.

Being an island tucked into a corner of the globe, New Zealand generally had a time and location advantage. However, Covid-19 had finally arrived on our shores and the number of confirmed cases in New Zealand had risen to five. According to the news reader, there was now a two-week self-isolation recommendation period for anyone entering the country.

Wait a minute. Two weeks of isolation? Uh oh. What would this mean for my parents who were planning to travel here soon?

CHAPTER 10

PRIDE IS A DIFFICULT PILL TO SWALLOW

If anyone were to ask me about the one thing that made my hospital stay stand out, it was the widespread prevalence of Covid-19 news. It was on TV almost every hour of the day, splattered across the different print, online and social media and discussed by everyone within earshot. Although the case numbers in New Zealand were low compared to the rest of the world, the rate of increase was exponential, a fact that was worrying hospital staff. They now had to prepare and brace themselves for a potential influx of Covid-19 patients alongside their normal duties. I take my hat off to all frontline health workers; their commitment and devotion to the tasks at hand never wavered. I was assured several times by different staff members that the oncology unit of a South Island hospital in New Zealand was, despite the looming threat, one of the safest places to be in.

Accommodation for friends and family when they came to visit us in New Zealand had never been an issue. It was an unspoken agreement that our doors were always open to anyone who visited. They could stay for as long as they wished (note: terms and conditions apply). However, Covid-19 was a novelty, and the isolation suggestion was a complete bombshell. The self-isolation period recommended to stop the spread of Covid-19 threw a spanner in the works of my parents' plans to visit. At my oncologist's advice, they were strongly urged to self-isolate away from us for two weeks to prevent any remote possibility of Covid-19 exposure. Chemotherapy was going to compromise my immune system and leave me vulnerable to even the tiniest of colds.

It would be silly to treat my cancer successfully only to have me die from Covid-19.

We decided that we needed to put my parents up in separate accommodation for two weeks upon their arrival in New Zealand before they travelled to our home. As much as I wanted my parents with me, I could not stop a small voice in my head from raising a concern. This unexpected turn was going to take yet another massive chunk out of our financial resources.

I knew that my parents would insist on covering the cost of their last-minute flights and accommodation, but I didn't want to place them under any additional financial burden. They were both retired and the currency exchange rate was not in their favour (the New Zealand dollar was worth approximately three times the Malaysian ringgit). Rod and I decided that we were going to need to deal with it. The resources we had borrowed to complete our home build would have to be redirected to fund their travel. The house could wait. Everything was going to work out just fine.

Chapter 10: Pride Is a Difficult Pill to Swallow

Little did I realise that God was going to use this opportunity to bless me and teach me a lesson at the same time.

Growing up, my parents had always taught me that our private lives were exactly that, private. Joyous events were marked with intimate celebrations to prevent flaunting or showing off, whereas difficulties were kept secret, partly because we cherished our privacy but mostly because we were taught not to trouble anyone with our personal problems. I was brought up with the belief that everyone had their own difficulties, and they didn't need to know about mine. I carried this belief with me to adulthood: in order to avoid being a burden to others, I kept everything to myself. My life was full of secrets.

It was with this mindset that I initially approached my illness and its side effects. My condition was my own load to carry and no one else's. I was determined to fight it and bear my own burden with only family and perhaps a few close friends (read: only the people who absolutely needed to know) by my side.

But God had a growth challenge for me.

It started out with a conversation with a mentor and friend, Ashley. I had spent the week prior to treatment reaching out to several close friends and family with the news of my condition, and Ashley was one of them. Ashley and I had previously scheduled a mentoring call for the end of March, a date that I was now unable to make because it would be right in the middle of chemotherapy treatments. I reached out to let her know I couldn't attend this video meeting, tell her my news, and to discuss our agreement. It was then that Ashley said six words that changed my perspective drastically.

"Amy," she said softly. "It's okay to ask for help."

I was taken aback. Defensive, even. I didn't need help.

"Amy," she said softly. "It's okay to ask for help." I was taken aback. Defensive, even. I didn't need help.

"If you start a GoFundMe page, I'd be happy to contribute to your fund and share it with my friends," she told me.

"I should be okay, but I'll let you know if I do. Thank you so much, Ashley."

After our call ended, I sat in silence for a while and reflected on our conversation.

Why did she tell me that? The fewer people I needed help from, the better, right? By not asking for help, I was being considerate of others, wasn't I?

That last question halted my thoughts in their tracks. I had thought I was being considerate, but I wasn't sure if that was the truth. Was I reluctant to disclose my condition to the public truly out of consideration for others or was it due to another reason? Why was I so reluctant to tell others and to ask for help?

Chapter 10: Pride Is a Difficult Pill to Swallow

As I sat on my hospital bed, the truth hit me like a ton of bricks. I'd been so blind, fooling myself into thinking that it was for the benefit of others, but the real reason was that I was a self-serving, egocentric person. It had been all about me.

It was **PRIDE**.

Pride had made me believe that I was a strong woman. I was proud to be independent and self-sufficient. If there ever was a period when I struggled, no one else apart from family and close friends knew. In fact, a good case in point was my long-suffering itch prior to this diagnosis, where even my own parents were unaware of how badly it affected me! My ego had grown so large that I had a well-put-together, collected and composed front to maintain. Anything less than that was a weakness I couldn't afford to share. It had never crossed my mind that this strength was a smoke screen for my pride.

This realisation quickly led to another: I was a coward. In my pride, I lacked the courage to humble myself and **ask** for help.

---

*This realisation quickly led to another: I was a coward. In my pride, I lacked the courage to humble myself and **ask** for help.*

Asking for help was scary. I'd accepted offers of help in the past, but actively asking for help was a different level altogether. It terrified me. Asking for help meant being vulnerable and intentionally pulling down the screen I'd always had. It required a different type of strength than I thought I possessed. It meant letting people know that I wasn't as in control of it all as I seemed to be on the outside and acknowledging I was struggling. It was terrifying because I'd always pictured myself as the one giving and sharing. Never did I envision myself on the requesting and receiving end.

It was an extremely difficult and humbling revelation that shook me to my core.

In theory, I knew that I had a much bigger family than just my own. I had a loving church family, true friends and an amazing community that I was a part of. Living out what I knew in theory, however, was tough. It had been easy to be a part of these communities when I had no need of their assistance. I was an independent member. I had lived **surrounded by** community instead of in and with community. I had not been invested in a way that interdependent living called for. My independence and strength, the traits I was proud of, were the very things that prevented me from truly being a part of these families.

It was a revelation and an opportunity for growth. I had two options. I could either: 1) continue as I'd always done and keep my pride or 2) swallow my pride and ask for help.

The mere thought of the latter option was painful and uncomfortable because it required an enormous amount of humility. However, it was also the path to a better version of myself. The decision was completely my own. Was I going to stick to the comfortable decision and sort it out myself, or was I going to stretch and ask for help?

Chapter 10: Pride Is a Difficult Pill to Swallow

I had a long, drawn-out internal battle with my ego. It was eye-opening, raw and absolutely soul-crushing. For the very first time in my life, I was able to look my own pride in the face, and I didn't like it at all. Not a single bit. It made me sick to my stomach to realise I'd been holding on to it for so long.

So, I did the one thing that I'd been excelling at since I was diagnosed: I wept. I asked God for forgiveness again. I'd been such an immature idiot. Despite everything, I knew that forgiveness had been granted and that God loved me. From then on, I resolved to grow and be a better follower of Christ.

After the tears abated, I called the one person I knew would help: Nikki. I had not seen or spoken to Nikki since our trip to South Korea. We made small talk for a few minutes before I told her why I'd called. Understandably, she was taken aback by my news.

"You have what?" she asked after a shocked silence.

"Hodgkin's," I replied. I filled her in on the details of my condition as Nikki was just as scientifically knowledgeable, if not more than I was. I spoke of my parents' plight and the expenses that we were going to incur to get them safely across continents, as well as the two-week recommended isolation. Nikki listened intently, only interrupting occasionally with the odd clarifying question.

I finished relaying my story and hesitated. It was crunch time. Was I really going to do this?

The next few seconds, although brief, felt to me like an eternity. The urge to keep my request to myself and retreat to my comfort zone was overwhelming. We didn't need the help.

I knew we would manage to scrape through somehow. But this wasn't about needing help. It was about being humble enough to ask for it so that our burden would be lighter.

I summoned all the courage I could muster and swallowed the massive lump in my throat.

"Nikki, could you do me a favour?" I asked.

"Sure. Anything at all," came her immediate reply.

My mouth was dry, but I forced myself to speak.

"Could you please help me set up a Givealittle page for our family to aid with expenses during this time? It would mean a lot to me if you could help manage the page so that I don't have to maintain or update it myself while I'm in hospital," I blurted out quickly.

It was one of the most uncomfortable things I'd ever done in my life. My insides squirmed, and there was a hollow pit in my stomach. At the same time, I felt a quiet sense of accomplishment and peace. Although it was small, I had taken one step closer to conquering my pride. All I had to do was get off my high horse and say the words. Whatever Nikki's answer, I was a better person for having asked the question.

"Of course I can! What would you like me to say the money will be used for?"

I was floored and humbled. It really was that simple. All this while, it was my own one-sided thoughts and pride that had stood in the way.

"It would mainly be used for any medical expenses and my parents' travel. Last-minute flight tickets are usually costly, and they need two weeks' accommodation in town

Chapter 10: Pride Is a Difficult Pill to Swallow

due to Covid. Additional resources will be used for our living expenses during the treatment and recovery period, especially with me not working. Plus, we don't know how long Rod will be able to take time off."

"Not a problem. I'll have it set up by the end of the day."

I thanked her profusely and we spoke for a few more minutes before I ended the call, citing weariness. That conversation had taken a massive amount of mental and emotional strength. Although the call had lasted less than 20 minutes, I'd had to wrestle with my whole being to verbalise the request.

Later that afternoon, Nikki sent me the link to the Givealittle page that she'd set up. Despite my big win, I knew that I had one more challenge to overcome. It was one thing to ask one person for help. It was another to ask the world. A crowdfunding effort like Givealittle wouldn't bear any fruit in the absence of a crowd. I had to step out of my comfort zone, tell people about my condition and ask them for help.

I decided that there was no time like the present, and I was done. I was done struggling by myself. I was done living an independent, but lonely life. I was ready to lean on God and others for help. I was ready to not be ashamed of it. In fact, there was nothing shameful about asking for help.

The first people I told about my decision were my parents. I explained that I believed this was the right thing to do. I shared the link with them and requested that they share it with their friends, our extended family, our church and our community. It was then up to individuals to either contribute to the cause or not. I made sure to emphasise that there was no obligation or pressure to contribute. The one thing I did solicit earnestly was prayer. I was going to need all the prayers that anyone was happy to offer. My parents, bless them, were extremely supportive of my decision. If they had misgivings, they did a really good job of hiding them.

I also decided to tell the world, and what better way to do it than on social media? I posted a public announcement on Facebook. It was part of my coming out. After all, we lived in an era where nothing was official until it was on Facebook. Even the level of commitment between two people was determined by whether or not their Facebook relationship status had been updated[25].

The response I received was overwhelming. Within seconds of putting the post up, the well wishes and kind messages started pouring in.

I was FLOORED.

Never in my wildest imagination could I have imagined the amount of support we got that single day. My family, relatives, friends, clients and people I had befriended or met at one point in my life rallied together to send me resources — their money and their time — from all over the world: New Zealand, The Netherlands, Malaysia and Australia, to name just a few countries. They sent me text messages, voice messages, recorded video messages, and most importantly,

---

25 *Things have changed recently, though, with TikTok dance videos taking the world by storm. I wonder how one can dance their way through a cancer announcement…*

prayers to God for me. My phone dinged with notifications all day long and kept dinging well into the night. It was constant and so frequent that I had to turn it on silent to get some sleep. The level of support filled me with an overwhelming sense of gratitude. And so, I did the only thing I was capable of at that moment.

I wept yet again. It was an ugly cry, with big, fat, heavy tears. It was a good thing I had a private room because I probably would have scared my roommate with my sobs. I wept tears of joy and freedom, finally realising what it feels like to have the weight of a heavy burden alleviated thanks to the support of many.

My cancer journey had barely begun, but I had already cried so many tears. This was going to be an enlightening, soul-cleansing experience.

Within 48 hours, the page had raised over $3000. What a blessing. God had come through yet again, this time with the help of His other children. He had wiped yet another thing off my 'worry' list. There truly was nothing God couldn't do.

All I had to do now was sit back, relax and go along for the ride.

CHAPTER 11

THE IMPORTANCE OF PREPARATION

Ever since I was little, I've hated cooking. It's not the cooking that I truly dislike, it's the preparation. Granny always told me that the prep work was just as important, if not more important, than the actual cooking itself. All the time-consuming activities: chopping, cutting, peeling, washing, cleaning. The actual food-meets-heat and raw-to-cooked process usually took less time than the prep. Despite my dislike for the preparation process, I know it's necessary as it makes cooking a lot easier. I can only imagine the time it would take to cook a whole carrot compared to the shredded bits.

Granny always told me that the prep work was just as important, if not more important, than the actual cooking itself.

The week prior to chemotherapy commencing was slow-moving. I knew that treatment couldn't begin before certain procedures took place and results were out, but intellectual knowledge of a fact did not equate to emotional and mental acceptance. There was, however, little I could do to speed up the passing of time, so I spent my days in the hospital resting in preparation for the battle ahead.

The 11th of March, a Wednesday, was when things started moving at double speed. I'd just had my routine blood test when another nurse entered with some news.

"You have a dental inspection this morning. The orderly will be here in a few minutes to wheel you over to the dental school."

She gestured to the window. "It's a little chilly outside, so it may pay to put another layer on."

I looked out the window. It was shaping up to be a sunny day, but it was still early, and the morning sun was barely peeking through the clouds. "Thank you for letting me know."

"You're welcome. The dental clinic is across the road, so you'll be leaving this building. We'll see you when you're back in an hour or so," she said before leaving the room.

No sooner had I pulled on my trusty pink woollen cardigan than the orderly arrived with a wheelchair. The sight of the wheelchair ruffled me; yet another one of many unnerving moments I experienced at the hospital. While I felt physically fine, there were constantly little hints and reminders throughout my days that I was a cancer patient. That this wasn't just the common cold. Truth is, I could have

Chapter 11: The Importance of Preparation

walked over to the dental clinic that day. However, there were procedures in place and as a cancer patient, this was one of them — I was to be wheeled over, regardless of whether or not I could walk.

I decided to take it on in good humour. After all, I had no plans to be wheeled around in the long run, so I might as well enjoy the ride while they were happy to do it.

The dental school was the first time I experienced what I now dub 'Covid discrimination'. Once we arrived at our destination, the orderly who had wheeled me over left for his other duties while I waited my turn in the patient waiting area. After filling out a form with my details, I was very politely asked by a senior dentist to don a face mask due to my coughing. Although I explained that my chronic cough was a side effect of my condition, I was still required to wear a face covering to protect the interests of the other patients, who were nervous about being around someone who coughed constantly.

Perturbed but understanding, I agreed. That interaction, however, made me realise that we were living in quite different times. The possibility that people may be discriminated against and sidelined for the mere act of coughing had never crossed my mind. I had no idea at the time, but it was a sign of things to come. At the time of writing, face masks are considered essential and a normal part of daily life. In fact, these days, their absence is considered an abnormality.

The dental check-up went by without a hitch. After a thorough X-ray and manual inspection, the dentist on duty declared my teeth and gums in overall good health. I was signed off to begin chemotherapy without requiring substantial oral work. To ease the tension at the end of the appointment (the dentist looked really sorry for me after reading over my notes and realising the reason for my thorough examination), I joked that it was unfortunate that straight, aligned teeth were not a prerequisite for chemotherapy. I could have done with some braces to straighten the misaligned rabbit teeth I've had for years.

It wasn't long after I got back (courtesy of another orderly who so kindly wheeled me back to my room) that I was notified of a lung capacity test. This time, I was wheeled down to a pulmonary function lab, where I was again made to fill in paperwork. Throughout my stay at the hospital, I filled in so many forms that I can recite my NHI (national health index) number by heart to this day. Being able to recall your NHI number isn't something to be happy about, as it means a certain amount of familiarity with a health identifier code and, by extension, considerable health services.

This lung test was to confirm that my lungs were healthy enough to undergo chemotherapy and to get a baseline reading of my lung capacity before treatment. It was to be repeated after my treatment was over to determine the effect of chemotherapy on the lungs. In my case, it was important to get the lung function test to determine if the tumour shrinking had a positive effect on my breathing capacity and to check if the chemotherapy drugs had a negative effect on the lungs. I was once again struck by how thorough the medical service was. Although things felt like they were moving really slowly

Chapter 11: The Importance of Preparation

at that time, looking back now, they really fast-tracked me through all the procedures, considering how busy and short staffed they were!

Later that evening, I was wheeled into the surgical room for my PICC line insertion. Dr Tim had come through for me again, managing to slot me in for an urgent procedure. I was immensely grateful to him as it was imperative that I got my central intravenous line. Without a PICC line, I wasn't able to begin chemotherapy because normal IV lines accessed via the veins in the crook of the elbow were considered insufficiently robust for chemotherapy infusions.

The doctor in charge was a young, attractive female with a kind smile. Although she was busy preparing her instruments, she kept a steady flow of conversation to keep my mind at ease.

"Do you know what the PICC line is for?" she asked, her eyes crinkled in a smile.

I nodded. "Dr Fiona explained it to me last week."

She gestured toward the flat surgical table, and I lay down on it. It was hard and unyielding. They certainly didn't design surgical tables for comfort.

"That's good. You will have no need for any other IV needles once we get this in, with one caveat. You will have to do your utmost best to keep the insertion site clean and sterile. If the site is infected, you may be at risk of a blood clot or infection. In that event, we'll need to withdraw the existing line and insert a brand-new one. As long as you take care of your line, it will last the length of your chemotherapy regime."

I silently vowed to be cautious with caring for my line and only have one for the duration of my treatment. I didn't want to have to go through this again!

Soon enough, I was draped with multiple surgical covers and told to angle my head to the side. The surgical drapes covered my whole upper torso, with only the underside of my arm exposed. The room was quiet save for the loud whirring of medical equipment. The lights in the room were switched off, replaced by bright surgical lights that were focused on the single spot on my arm. All the medical staff in the room were donned from head to toe in safety equipment, looking like knights from the mediaeval times with their suits of armour on, presumably to protect them from being exposed to excessive radiation from these daily procedures. I experienced a brief moment of admiration for medical professionals. They truly sacrificed a lot to serve others.

"We'll be using imaging technology to visualise the vein in your arm. Once we find a good one, we'll give it a little nick, insert this catheter into your vein, and we'll be done. Easy peasy." The doctor showed me the length of catheter tubing that she held in her hands.

"Sounds simple enough to me," I agreed with a smile.

"We'll give you some local anaesthetic now and begin in a few minutes once you have lost sensation in your arm," she said.

I felt the sharp prick of a needle and winced. Better a needle than a surgical knife.

Chapter 11: The Importance of Preparation

After a few minutes, my arm was numb. Despite the absence of pain, the sensations I experienced were strange. My arm felt like it was being forcefully pushed, prodded and tugged. It was grossly uncomfortable. I was secretly glad my vision was obscured. Throughout the procedure, I was aware of another doctor squeezing my hand reassuringly. I was immensely grateful for his support during this unnerving procedure.

"And … we're done!" the female doctor exclaimed. In a flourish, the surgical drapes were removed from my torso and wrapped into a little bundle. As the bundle was tossed into the nearby medical bin, I spotted a blood and iodine-drenched cover.

Ugh. I averted my eyes, sat up on the table and glanced down at my arm.

There was a neat cloth bandage wrapped around my right bicep. The doctor smiled at me, no longer wearing her protective equipment.

"You have nice veins. That was a straightforward insertion."

She handed me a laminated card the size of a credit card.

"This is your catheter ID card. Make sure you carry this around with you in your wallet for identification in the event of a medical emergency. It gives them information on the presence and location of your PICC line, which will allow quick and instant access to an IV line. Your arm will probably start throbbing in a few minutes once the anaesthetic wears off. Make sure you keep on top of the pain relief. Paracetamol will help. Don't wait until it starts hurting before asking for pills because they take a while to start working. Do you have any questions?"

I shook my head and swung my legs off the table. "Thank you for that."

She helped me back to my hospital bed, which had been parked in a corner during my procedure. "Not a problem. All the best with your treatment."

That afternoon, after several doses of paracetamol, I posted my first Facebook update with a victory image of my bandaged bicep — which I'd fondly dubbed my 'Popeye arm'. In fact, I had a leg up on Popeye. I hadn't had to inhale a whole can of spinach to get my biceps. Plus, I didn't even need one on each side. All I needed was one arm. With one arm, I was now well on my way to conquering cancer. Go me!

The multiple tests and procedures had taken a lot out of me, and I spent the next day recovering. The cloth bandage was soon removed to reveal a neat, waterproof dressing with a protruding plastic nozzle taped to the surface. This nozzle was the new access site to my veins, and the nurses, who were careful not to disturb my rest, now had an easy avenue to draw blood for my routine tests. I was provided with a plastic sleeve during showers that protected the site and the dressing from water. All in all, things were moving along rather nicely.

Chapter 11: The Importance of Preparation

12th of March 2020. Thursday evening

"You need to fly in now or it might be too late," I said, frustrated at my inability to get through to my parents. We were on a video call, and my parents had just given me some unexpected news.

My mum had a full-blown cold: a runny nose, red eyes, a nasty cough and terrible sneezes — the whole nine yards. It was obviously a side effect of stress from hearing my news and lack of sleep. Her body, unused to such a level of stress, was caving due to the pressure. My brother and I had been in contact over the past week, and he'd confided in me that she wasn't taking the news well. She was calm only when on calls with me, keeping her emotions in check so as not to distress me further.

"If you don't come now, you might not get an opportunity for a while," I repeated exasperatedly.

Covid-19 was not doing us any favours. Due to the widespread occurrence of the disease and the fear that now accompanied a Covid infection, any seemingly related symptom was not well tolerated in public. My own experience at the dental school was proof. Given the discrimination, my parents didn't want to risk being barred from the airport or their flight. There was no precedent for this, and nothing was official (yet), but there had been news reports of several airlines taking matters into their own hands by preventing passengers with Covid-like symptoms from boarding.

"The only way to be allowed to fly is a negative Covid test. I'm sure your mum only has a cold, so we don't want to risk waiting at a testing centre with potentially hundreds of Covid-positive cases. The risk of contracting Covid by doing that is extremely high. We've discussed this and decided it's best to let her cold run its course before we head your way," my dad told me.

I shook my head repeatedly in exasperation. How was I going to get them to understand that it was now or not for a long time? Covid was spreading rapidly, causing thousands of deaths a day, and decisions were made on what seemed like an hourly basis. The USA had already closed their borders to Asian countries, and I had a feeling that New Zealand was soon going to head in that direction. At present, the timing was perfect — in fact, flight tickets were going for a fraction of their normal price to induce people to fly as most people were cancelling their travel plans in favour of the safety of home.

My dad sighed and continued, "We may not even be allowed to board the plane at the airport. Your mum is extremely symptomatic and at the moment people are staring and complaining at the slightest hint of a sniff or cough. It's disturbing."

"I understand, Dad. But I really think it's worth a shot. There's nothing legally barring you from boarding or flying. If the worst happens and you're prevented from boarding, then so be it. At least we tried."

"Yes, we understand, but we're also worried about catching Covid in transit. Our utmost priority is you, and we don't want to put you at any additional risk."

Chapter 11: The Importance of Preparation

"But that's what the isolation is for! We'll put you up for two whole weeks, more if needed, in a hotel room. Once the fourteen days are over and you're all clear, at least then we'll be in the same country!"

But my parents were adamant. They had made their minds up not to expose me to any additional risk, especially in my vulnerable condition. The lack of concrete information also added to their concerns — it was barely three weeks prior that the WHO announced an official seven-day isolation period for the virus. In a span of a few days, the official advice had increased the isolation duration to double the original period. It was anyone's guess as to when or what would change next. The novel virus had taken the world by surprise, and officials were scrambling to accumulate as much information as they could in a short amount of time.

I tried one last time.

"Dad, this is going to be around for a while. Are you sure you don't want to just give it a try? The worst thing that can happen is you get turned away at the airport."

"We're sure. Don't worry, Amy. We'll be there before you know it. This whole virus saga will blow over soon — look at what happened with MERS and SARS. Things died down pretty quickly then, too. Once this ends, we'll fly over as soon as we can."

I wasn't convinced, but I respected their decision. Although my parents weren't going to be physically present, I took comfort from the fact that they would be well and safe as long as they stayed where they were. The odds of contracting the virus on a flight were higher than if they stayed home.

I'm usually pretty happy and chuffed when I'm proven right; Rod will be able to attest to that. However, this time was different. When the news aired that same afternoon, my heart sank to the pit of my stomach. This was one occasion I'd really hoped that I was going to be wrong.

It was official: WHO had declared Covid-19 to be a pandemic. It was going to be a problem for the whole world for a long time. True to my prediction, six days after that conversation with my parents, the New Zealand borders were closed to all but New Zealand citizens and permanent residents.

So much for blowing over.

CHAPTER 12

THE END OF THE BEGINNING

It was perplexing, considering my circumstances, but the quiet days prior to the start of chemotherapy were a few of the most peaceful days of my life. Physically, all my needs were met. Emotionally and spiritually, I had never been better. The long six-month journey of cancer discovery was drawing to a close, and alongside cancer, I'd found myself again. I'd rediscovered my identity as God's child, and I'd never been more certain of who I was in Him. That revelation, in turn, flowed into my relationships with my husband, my children, my parents, my family and my friends — I was a better wife, mother, daughter and friend. Ironically, life had never been better.

However, there were a few loose ends to tie up before the close of this chapter and the beginning of the next. Friday marked an important day of this transition period as I secured what was going to be a staple in my life from then on: a gorgeous wig. One of my nurses had given me information on a wig provider whose service was excellent. She met me in the hospital ward with several samples for me to try and test. At her urging and to the disappointment of quite a few of my friends, I decided against bubblegum-pink and instead chose a synthetic, bob length, auburn brown wig. The cost of the wig was partially funded by the health system, so all I had to do was pay for the portion not covered by the subsidy. This was where I used a small portion of the Givealittle funds — it was incredible how costly artificial hair was.

After leaving me with some valuable wig care tips — note to self: do not stand too close to direct heat, such as an open fire or the oven door or the wig will singe — she left me admiring my own reflection in the mirror. I'd chosen well. The wig I'd selected made me look absolutely spiffy. After I shaved my head, Lucas and Holly would always quip that they knew we were about to head out to town when "Mummy put her hair on!" For months after my treatment, the wig was my makeup or dress up equivalent.

For months after my treatment, the wig was my makeup or dress up equivalent.

Throughout my hospital stay, I also had a steady stream of well-wishing visitors. My in-laws, my church family, friends and neighbours brought me a steady supply of treats, chocolates, flowers, home-cooked meals and small pamper items such as fragrant-smelling toiletries. These little touches

Chapter 12: The End of the Beginning

added a homely feel to my stay in the otherwise bare and sterile room. Rod visited every two to three days, bringing with him a bag of his clean T-shirts each time. I preferred wearing normal day-to-day clothing instead of the hospital gown but found that his oversized, baggy T-shirts were more comfortable than my own outfits. My poor husband found himself with fewer T-shirts throughout the whole treatment period; it was a good thing he had quite a few.

One of my many visitors was someone I'd not expected to see. He knocked on the door and poked his head through the privacy curtains at my acknowledgement. To my great surprise, it was Dr John. It turned out that his office at the hospital was on the same floor and that he'd heard about my condition through Dr Adam.

"Dr John!" I exclaimed. "I didn't expect to see you here!" I gave him a small wave from my seat on the hospital bed.

He eased his long body into the room and sat in the chair by my bed. "Dr Adam told me about your diagnosis. Who would have thought that your itch was a symptom of Hodgkin's?"

I smiled. "No one could have guessed. Even Dr Fiona, my haematologist, said that it's one of the rarer symptoms."

Dr John smiled back sadly. "I'm sorry I couldn't do much to help you, but you didn't present with any other symptoms during our consultations."

"Well, I'm really glad you came by," I replied. "Thank you for not caving in and prescribing me another course of prednisone when I asked for it. Now that I'm on oral medication, I've realised that prednisone is one of the drugs used to shrink the tumour. Had you written me the script, I would have been on steroids and the collection on my clavicle would have potentially been obscured for a lot longer, which would have delayed my diagnosis."

And it would have. There were already various news reports on delayed non-essential diagnostic testing and imaging due to the increasing spread of Covid-19 in the country. If I had been on steroids, I wouldn't have had the lump, and I wouldn't have paid for the ultrasound. Consequently, I wouldn't have had the quick diagnosis. Had we been delayed by even a week or chosen to wait on the public roll for the ultrasound, my ultrasound would have been classified as a non-essential procedure. It could have cost me my life.

Yet another score for God using our decisions for good.

I also received a surprise call from the dermatology department in Dunedin that Friday. I answered my phone with a questioning "Hello?" because I didn't recognise the number that flashed on my screen. It turned out that it was a booking coordinator calling from the dermatologist's office about the specialist referral that Dr Adam had put in weeks ago. They were finally ready to see me. Before she could explain further and find me some dates, I interrupted her.

"Thank you so much for calling, but I don't need this appointment anymore."

"You don't?" she echoed.

Chapter 12: The End of the Beginning

"No, I'm actually in the hospital. It turned out that the rash and skin condition I was suffering from was a symptom of Hodgkin's lymphoma. I'm in the oncology ward right at this very moment."

There was a small gasp. "Oh no, I'm so sorry to hear that!"

I smiled. "It's all good. No one knew and I don't know if the dermatologist would have picked up on it either. It's perhaps good to note down on the record, though, that a rash such as mine could be a symptom of something more ominous like cancer."

"I will definitely pass that on to our dermatologists! I'm sorry to hear about your diagnosis, but all the best with your treatment, and apologies we couldn't get you in sooner."

I thanked her and hung up.

"It's either stage four or stage two with B symptoms — which means that other organs are involved. We also couldn't quite classify the exact type of Hodgkin's lymphoma because we had to settle for the punch biopsy instead of a general surgery one," Dr Fiona explained. "However, the exact classification doesn't matter, as we've decided that the best regime for you is the escalated-BEACOPP[26] cycle."

---

[26] *BEACOPP is an acronym for the drugs bleomycin sulfate (B), etoposide phosphate (E), doxorubicin hydrochloride (Adriamycin, A), cyclophosphamide (C), vincristine sulfate (Oncovin, O), procarbazine hydrochloride (P) and prednisone (P). I've added some additional information on this treatment to the resources section.*

It was the end of the week, and my whole medical team had just filed into my room to deliver the news. Rod was by my side.

Dr Fiona handed me a sheet of paper with a summary of the treatment in diagram form. She pointed to different portions of the diagram with a pen while she continued (note: the diagram is attached to the resources section).

"Each cycle of the treatment takes three weeks. You'll undergo two cycles of BEACOPP, followed by a PET/CT scan. These first two cycles will be the main ones that kill the cancer cells. The following cycles function to mop up any remaining cancer cells. The PET/CT scan after the first two cycles will determine how many 'mop up cycles' you need. If your scan comes up hot, you will need another four cycles of BEACOPP, which means a total of six cycles. This is the full regime. The maximum number of cycles we give a patient is six. However, if your PET/CT scan comes back cold, you will only need another two cycles of BEACOPP, which makes a total of only four cycles. Regardless of whether you have four or the full six, you'll have a final PET/CT scan at the end of the treatment plan to make sure all is well. If the scan still comes back positive after six cycles, then we will discuss the option of localised radiation for any present residual lymphoma tissue."

I nodded as my eyes followed the progress of her pen along the paper. It sounded simple enough.

"Have you been given all the information on chemotherapy?"

Chapter 12: The End of the Beginning

I had indeed. The nurse had come by that week with a folder full of information. There were books, leaflets and articles on side effects, advice and suggestions, as well as information on support networks available for patients. As information-driven as I was, I'd only leafed through most of the material. All the information was mainly on negative side effects, and I'd decided after reading through one page that I didn't want my cancer journey to be marred by someone else's. I refused to be predisposed to think that things were going to be awful when I hadn't personally gone through it yet.

I was going to take things as they came. As far as I was concerned, I had an 'infection' that the doctors were going to treat with 'antibiotics'. I was well equipped: the IV line that had been inserted was a surefire way to deliver the 'antibiotics' directly into the blood system. As long as I was a good patient and completed the course of 'antibiotics' prescribed to me, I was going to be cured of my 'infection'. As for how I would respond to the 'antibiotics' — everyone was different. Some people responded better to 'antibiotics' than others. My response was in no way dependent on anyone else's. My journey was going to be my own.

My response was in no way dependent on anyone else's. My journey was going to be my own.

"Yes, I have. I only looked through them briefly, but I think I got the gist of things," I replied.

"Good. There are just several important points I'd like to speak with you about. Firstly, you will need to tell me immediately if you suffer from any numbness or tingling in your fingers or toes. If you have difficulty with fine motor skills such as doing up buttons, inform us immediately. Some drugs in your regime can cause nerve damage, but this effect is preventable as long as we monitor and tailor the dose to suit you."

"Right, tingling or numbness in the extremities. Got it," I said, making a mental note.

"Secondly, the bleomycin in your treatment can cause lung damage and respiratory distress particularly if you're given high levels of oxygen. If you are hospitalised for any reason during your treatment due to a trauma, tell your medical team that you're undergoing the BEACOPP cycle. The oxygen that is usually provided to patients to aid their breathing will in fact, cause you harm."

"Oh, good to know. I'll remember that." I had no intention of intentionally experiencing a traumatic incident, but accidents could happen, and this was potentially information that could save my life.

The last side effect that Dr Fiona wanted to discuss came in the form of a question. "Do you want more children?"

"Nope, we're done."

I looked at my husband and we both chuckled — we had both answered her at the exact same time. Rod had

Chapter 12: The End of the Beginning

been the quiet observer up until this point, absorbing all the information that Dr Fiona shared.

Dr Fiona smiled. "Great minds. Are you sure?" she asked, half-teasing, half-serious. "This treatment will render you infertile. If you would like to have more children in the future, we need to know now so that we can harvest and freeze your eggs prior to commencing treatment."

Wow. All I could do in that moment was marvel at God's timing. He had seen it fit to bless me with two pregnancies in quick succession (Lucas and Holly are 17 months apart in age). At the time, I wondered about the wisdom of having two children so close in age; we had barely gotten Lucas to sleep through the night when Holly was born, which meant that we had close to three consecutive years of sleepless nights in total. But God obviously knew because our little family became complete when Holly arrived. All I needed to do now was trust that He was going to use our circumstances for good, regardless of whether or not I was going to survive this particular challenge.

I looked at Rod, who smiled and nodded emphatically. I turned back to look at Dr Fiona. "Yes, we're very happy with our two. We won't need to extract my eggs."

"Okay, we can start your treatment soon then. That covers most things. Do you have any questions?"

I shook my head. "Not off the top of my head; the information I've been given is pretty thorough."

"Your treatment will start on Monday morning, so get as much rest as you can this weekend."

She gave me a small wave, and the whole medical team filed out the door after her.

The weekend passed quietly. On Friday evening, my work colleagues from the pool took me out for dinner in town, a meal that I will always remember as 'The Last Supper'. Ours was, however, an upgraded version compared to Jesus's last meal with His disciples prior to the crucifixion: we had pizza and drinks instead of unleavened bread and wine. Rod and the kids visited on Saturday, and I spent Sunday watching TV, reading my Bible and praying for the week ahead.

Soon enough, Monday morning came around. The sun rose early, signalling a nice, sunny day. I had an early breakfast and shower in anticipation of the long day ahead. At approximately ten in the morning, the nurse on duty knocked on the door and entered the room carrying two large infusion bags. She hung both bags up on the portable IV pole standing next to my bed.

"Amy!" she exclaimed. "We have your first chemotherapy infusion here for you. Let's get you started and kick this thing in the butt."

She looked at me closely with a kind smile. "Are you ready?"

I closed my Bible, set it gently on the table next to me and returned her smile. "Yes, I am."

AFTERWORD

Two years later, 2022

I'm sitting at my desk, typing away at the computer, the sun filtering through the window, when Holly comes bouncing excitedly into the room for her morning cuddle. I told her recently that mummies are just like cell phones and that we need daily 'charging' (read: cuddles). Since then, she has been an avid mummy charger. "Mummy loooooves charging!" she'll say while giving me a tight squeeze.

This morning, she has a different thing to say. "Mummy, your hair is all curly." She giggles, touching my soft curls with her fingers.

I smile. It isn't my fancy wig she's referring to. My hair has grown back, with a distinct wave compared to my pre-cancer straight locks.

Many other things have changed as well. I've officially been in remission since September 2020. Granny, whom I last saw on that visit in 2019, caught Covid and passed away peacefully in June 2021. My parents are finally visiting this year; two and a half years after my confirmed diagnosis. My relationship with God is growing daily, and although I still feel like a spiritual infant, I know that He is patient and loves me as long as I do my best.

A lot has happened in these past two years, and I probably haven't seen the end of the consequences of my cancer and subsequent treatment. That story, however, in my humble opinion, is a tale best left for another time.

You may find the ending of this book incredibly frustrating for many reasons, not the least of which is the desire to find out what the actual treatment and recovery journey was like. If you fall into that category, all I can say is this: God may one day move me to write a separate volume that narrates that journey in detail.

This journey of self-discovery was truly only the beginning. The person I am today is a more mature individual compared to the one I've written about in this book. However, I still have a lot of room to learn and grow daily. God willing, I'd be happy to bring you on the continuation of my journey in a separate book.

If my story has moved or inspired you in any way, I'd love to hear from you.

RESOURCES

Identity Framework

For more information on the framework Amy has on finding your identity, please visit: AmyEwald.com/FindingMeResources

Coaching

For more information on identity coaching and to experience a coaching session with Amy, please visit:

AmyEwald.com

BONUS: Receive a gifted coaching session with your purchase of this book. Visit AmyEwald.com/FindingMeResources

Connect

Write to Amy at AmyEwald.com

OR

Reach out via social media: Facebook.com/amy.hoo.ewald/

AN OVERVIEW OF MY TREATMENT PLAN

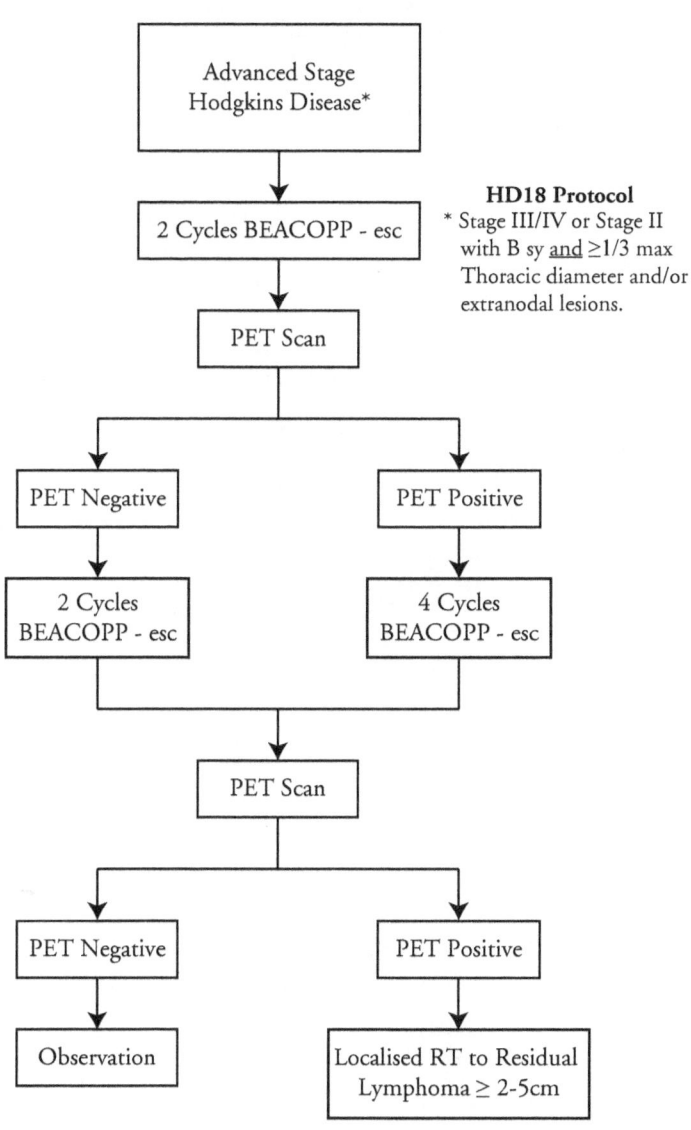

An overview of the escalated-BEACOPP treatment schedule: Taken from the Cancer Institute NSW site[27]

Cycle 1 to 6

Drug	Dose	Route	Day
Prednisolone	40 mg/m² ONCE a day	PO	1 to 14
Procarbazine	100 mg/m² ONCE a day	PO	1 to 7
DOXOrubicin	35 mg/m²	IV	1
CYCLOPHOSPHamide	1,250 mg/m²	IV infusion	1
Etoposide *	200 mg/m²	IV infusion	1 to 3
Pegfilgrastim **	6 mg	Subcut	4
vinCRISTine	1.4 mg/m²(Cap dose at 2 mg)	IV infusion	8
Bleomycin	10,000 International Units/m²	IV	8

* *Etopophos (etoposide phosphate) 113.6 mg is equivalent to etoposide 100 mg. Doses in this protocol are expressed as etoposide.*

** *Pegfilgrastim or equivalent G-CSF (filgrastim, lenograstim or lipegfilgrastim) can be used. Monitor patients closely for signs of pulmonary toxicity as the combination of bleomycin and G-CSF may increase the risk of bleomycin induced pulmonary toxicity.*

Frequency:

21 days

Cycles:

6

---

27 https://www.eviq.org.au/haematology-and-bmt/lymphoma/hodgkin-lymphoma/1461-beacopp-escalated-bleomycin-etoposide-doxoru

ACKNOWLEDGEMENTS

This has been a long journey, one which I could not have completed without the help and support of many people who deserve to be acknowledged. So many people have helped me on this journey that I may not be able to name them all. If your name is not listed, please know that I appreciate you too.

Firstly, to you, dear reader. Thank you so much for your support and for reading my story.

To my coaches, Eugenia Marembo and Ruth Saw, thank you for being my anchors. I am extremely grateful for your suggestions, advice and unwavering support.

My brother in Christ and friend, Lance Mosher, thank you for sharing your experience, all the words of wisdom, advice and suggestions, and for cheering me on. I could not have completed this book without your input.

Melissa Prideaux, for your editing expertise, thank you so much for your hard work and support. Your command of the English language and your many ideas have been an immense help; I am so grateful I found you.

Sarah Johnson for designing the cover and Praditha Kahatapitiya the layout and typesetting; this book wouldn't be as gorgeous as it is without you both!

My beta readers and launch team, thank you for your willingness, your support and your time in helping me market this book. My efforts would have been in vain without readers, and you played a massive part in getting this book into the hands of those who would read it.

To my immediate, extended and church family, thank you for your unwavering love, support and guidance. You have all always stood by me, believed in me and continually encouraged me with your love and support. I honestly could not have completed this project without you.

To my husband, Rod, I will be eternally grateful to you for putting up with my crazy hours of writing and working. You work just as many, if not more, hours to support our family, our dreams and our lifestyle, and you do it without complaining and with so much love. I love you so much.

Finally, to God, without Whom none of this would have been possible — may I be reminded of your love daily and continue to strive to serve you faithfully for as long as I live.

ABOUT THE AUTHOR

Amy Ewald (PhD) is an author, coach and speaker who believes that every single person on this earth has been uniquely and wonderfully made. Having found her identity through a challenging cancer diagnosis, Amy is passionate about helping people uncover their identity, live out the good lives they are meant to have, and be the person God created them to be. She lives in New Zealand with her husband, Rod, and their two young children. In her spare time, she can be found either reading a good book, writing an equally good book, watching a Korean drama (they're great!) or spending quality time with her family.

www.ingramcontent.com/pod-product-compliance
Lightning Source LLC
Chambersburg PA
CBHW022055290426
44109CB00014B/1107